India Antiquarian Dept Bhavnagar

Corpus Inscriptionum Bhavnagari

Being a Selection of Arabic and Persian Inscriptions

India Antiquarian Dept Bhavnagar

Corpus Inscriptionum Bhavnagari
Being a Selection of Arabic and Persian Inscriptions

ISBN/EAN: 9783743330351

Manufactured in Europe, USA, Canada, Australia, Japa

Cover: Foto ©ninafisch / pixelio.de

Manufactured and distributed by brebook publishing software
(www.brebook.com)

India Antiquarian Dept Bhavnagar

Corpus Inscriptionum Bhavnagari

CORPUS INSCRIPTIONUM BHAVNAGARI:

BEING

A SELECTION

OF

ARABIC AND PERSIAN INSCRIPTIONS

COLLECTED BY THE

ANTIQUARIAN DEPARTMENT,

BHAVNAGAR STATE.

EDITED DURING THE RULE OF

H. H. THE MAHARAJA SIR TAKHTSINGHJI, G.C.S.I.

Bombay:
PRINTED AT THE
EDUCATION SOCIETY'S STEAM PRESS, BYCULLA.
1889.

PREFACE.

For some years past His Highness Maharaj Sir Takhtsinghji, G. C. S. I., of Bhavnagar, having felt the want of an organized agency to collect materials for the past history of Bhavnagar, sanctioned in A. D. 1881 the establishment of a Department for an Archæological and Antiquarian Survey—the first of its kind started in Kathiawad—at the suggestion of the late Colonel J. W. Watson, then President of the Rajasthanic Court in Kathiawad, who was well-known for his tastes in these researches; who possessed an excellent knowledge of Persian; and who by his keen and constant interest in the progress of this work rendered most valuable assistance, which has put this Department under his everlasting obligation. Since A. D. 1882 Pandits have been sent on exploring tours in different parts of Kathiawad, Gujarat, Marwar, Mewar, &c., and the result of the researches carried on during the last eight years has been the accumulation of a pretty extensive stock of old and (some of them) unique coins, and fac-similes of stone and copper-plate inscriptions, relating not merely to the Gohel chiefs of the past, for whose past history the Department was first started, but to other rulers and places. General Sir A. Cunningham, late Director General of the Archæological Survey of India, one of the greatest Indian Archæologists, has expressed as his opinion that these inscriptions are the most certain and the most trustworthy authority for determining the dates of Indian monuments. Besides it is a well-known fact that researches in Indian Archæology and Epigraphy have received a fresh stimulus of late. It was, therefore, decided at the desire of His Highness that the best way to turn the collection to account for the use of scholars and antiquarians would be to publish a selection of the inscriptions in parts from time to time. In compliance with this desire this selection has been prepared containing some fifty-one inscriptions in Arabic and Persian, collected from different places and extending over a period of seven centuries, viz., from 591 A. H. to 1291 A. H. The text given was prepared from impressions of the original with the help of experts and were then rendered into English aswell as into Gujarati; and each of the transcripts is preceded by a short introduction and is followed by its translation into English. In several places the text is either illegible, obscure, doubtful, or incorrect. It is to be hoped, however, that these lithic records will prove highly useful to persons interested in the history and philology of the Mahomedans in Gujarat and Kathiawad. As this small volume is intended for those who have real interest in the matter, it will be gratifying to the Bhavnagar Durbar as well as to those who have participated in its preparation if the work done by them is appreciated by those students of Indian history and antiquities, and especially of the province of Kathiawad.

I must not here omit to state that this Department acknowledges with great thanks the valuable help rendered in preparing this small volume by Mr. Burjorji Ardesir Enti, B. A., Professor in the Samaldas College, Munshi Hussanally Gulamally, of Bhavnagar High School and Munshi Shekh Mahomed Isphani, of Samaldas College.

VAJESHANKER GOURISHANKER OZA.

BHAVNAGAR, 15th May 1889.

CONTENTS.

ii   CONTENTS.

PERSIAN & ARABIC INSCRIPTIONS.

STONE INSCRIPTION AT GOGHÂ.

Dated A.H. 591.

The stone containing this inscription is raised under an *Ambli* tree grown on the side of the way leading to the shrine of Pirânpir on the sea-beach at Goghâ, a British port in the Gulf of Cambay on the east coast of Kâthiâvâd. It contains five lines written in Arabic characters. It measures 18" × 15", and mentions the death of a martyr named Bâbâ Taju-ud-din in A.H. 591, A.D. 1195. The stone is the common sand-stone, but well preserved.

تختي اول

1 — بسم الله الرحمن الرحيم لا اله الا الله محمد رسول الله

2 — كل من عليها فان و يبقى وجہ ربك ذوالجلال والاكرام

3 — انتقل من دارالفنآ الى دارالبقآ مفتخرالرجال

4 — السعيد الشہيد المظما (المظلوم ا) لمغفور با با تاج ا

5 — لدين بن بدرالدين شہر في ربيع الاخر سنه ٥٩١ه

In the name of God, the merciful and compassionate.

There is no god but God ; Mahomed is the prophet of God.

Every creature which lives on the earth is subject to decay ; but the glorious and honourable countenance of thy Lord shall remain for ever.

Bâbâ Taju-ud-din, son of Badr-ud-din, honoured by men ; fortunate, martyred, the oppressed, forgiven (by God), migrated from this house of destruction to that of eternity, in the month of Rabi-ul-âkhir A.H. 591.

1

STONE INSCRIPTION AT MÂNGAROL.

Dated A.H. 700.

This inscription is placed in an open room near the eastern gate at Mângarol, where the sepoy-guard is kept. Mângarol is a small sea-port town on the west coast of Kâthiâvâd. The stone is a piece of white marble measuring 16″ × 12″ with fourteen lines of Persian mentioning the building of the town wall by the Deputy Governor of Sorath, Malik Shekh-bin-Taj. It is dated A.H. 700, A.D. 1301.

---

1 ــ بسم الله الرحمن الرحیم

كه مثلش نشد درجهان شهريار — 2 ــ بعهد شهنشاه گيتي مدار

همهٔ خسروان بر درش برده وار — 3 ــ جهانگير زربتخش قلعر كشا

ز جودش جهان درجهان شرمسار — 4 ــ زعدلش سراسر جهان شادمان

بگجرات بد مقطع كامكار — 5 ــ زشهر خان اعظم ظفر خان وجیر

چو آصف بدانش چو رستم بكار — 6 ــ بتقوی چو عثمان چو حيدر بتيغ

ملك بدر بنجهل امير كبار — 7 ــ ز خان بود نایب بسورتهر همی

ابد در جهان دائیما با وقار — 8 ــ كريمي نكو راي روشن ضمير

جواني جوانصرد رعنا سوار — 9 ــ وزو بود نایب بمنگلور خوش

بر آمد بمنگلور رومي حصار (روئين) — 10 ــ ملك شيخ بن تاج كزسعي او

همه كس ثناگو بشهر و ديار — 11 ــ همه خلق خرسند از الطاف او

چه غم گر بيايد عدو صد هزار — 12 ــ بناه قوي گشت مر خانرا

زتاريخ هفصد شده در شمار — 13 ــ زهجرت نبوي (كم) شد ختم (اينتختار)

و زو ماند این سالها یاد گار — 14 ــ علا صدر خوش كرد تاريخ را

In the name of God, the merciful and compassionate.

In the reign of the emperor of the circle of the world; the like of whom there never was any king in the world; the gold-bestowing conqueror of the world, the opener of fortresses; before whose gate all kings were like slaves; owing to whose justice the world was altogether happy, whose liberality put the whole world to shame ; the great lord Zefer Khan, Vajih-ul-Mulk, was the absolute political officer of the Emperor in the province of Gujrat ; in piety like Osman ; in bearing sword like Khalif Haidar ; in wisdom like Asaf ; in war like Rustom.

This Khan had a deputy also in Sorath, (called) Malik Bedr Benjehel, the great nobleman ; generous, wise, of an enlightened heart ; always honoured in the world.

In Mângalor (Mângrol), he had a deputy, youthful, brave, and an admirable rider, (viz.) Malik Shekh bin Taj ; owing to whose exertions a Roman fortress was erected in Mângalore (Mângrol) ; all the people are pleased with his generosity ; everybody is praising him, in the town as well as in the country ; it became a great protection to the Khan ; no cause of fear even if a hundred thousand enemies were to rise.

* * * By calculation it is 700 A.H.

Ala Sadra has depicted this date, and its memory was preserved for many years on account of him.

STONE INSCRIPTION AT UNÂ.

Dated A.H. 708.

The stone in which this inscription is cut is built up in a wall of the Rozâ of Hazarat Pir at Unâ, a small town under Junâgadha State on the south coast of Kâthiâvâd. It is a yellow sand-stone measuring 30″ × 19″ with nine lines in Persian character. Some of the letters are very difficult to decipher. It mentions the building of a house of pilgrimage in honour of one Mahomed Asher in the time of Emperor Firoz Shah in A.H. 708, A.D. 1308-09.*

حو العلام

خدا ایكان فلک منزلت سلیمان جاه	1ـ بعهد دولت فرخنده بهتر عصر
جهان پناه زحل بارگاه ظل الاه	2ـ ابو المظفر فیروز شاه جهانگیر
بسلک طاعتش اصحاب دین نهند روىا	3ـ بملک او همر بقعات خیر شد معمور
بر این بهشت زیارت که بنده درگاه	4ـ بجارده زمئ و ده بسال هفتصد هشت
خطاب کرده ظفرخان مظفرحضرت شاه	5ـ محمد اشهر و لقمئ تا میرسیرت اخترش
بنا کرده بتوفیق این منور بارگاه	6ـ امیدوار بیاید دعائی نماید
این بهشت خوش بمان تا بود سپهروخورماه	7ـ همیشه باد آباد این خلدبرین بر زمین
امین رب العالمین	

---

* This date is doubtful as Sultan Firoz Shah ascended the throne of Delhi in A.D. 1351.

4

He is the Knower.

In the happy reign and good time of Abul 'Muzeffer Firoz Shah, the lord of heavenly dignity, of Solomon-like pomp, the conqueror of the world, whose court was as sublime as that of Saturn, the shadow of God ; in his kingdom good places were made ; religious men bow their faces by way of his worship ; on the 14th of the 10th month of 708. If any expectant comes to this paradise of pilgrimage of Mahomed Asher, the slave of God, possessed of the virtue of Lakman and of star-like nature, he will offer a blessing ; this Hazrat Shah (Mahomed Asher) gave the title of Muzeffer to Zeffer Khan. This brilliant presence hall was made by the grace of God. May this highest heaven on earth flourish for ever ! May this pleasant paradise last as long as the sky, the sun, and the moon (endure)!

O ! nourisher of the people of the world ! Be it so !

STONE INSCRIPTION IN THE MOSQUE OF PÂNAWÂDI AT PÂTANA IN KÂTHIÂVÂD.

Dated A.H. 720.

This inscription is cut in a white marble slab, whose surface measures 82" × 10". It is built up in one of the walls of the mosque which is in a garden called *Pânawâdi* near the celebrated temple of Somanâtha at Pâtana, also called Prabhâsa Pâtana, under Junâgadh, on the south-west coast of Kâthiâvâd. The inscription is written in only two lines of Persian character, mentioning the erection of the mosque by Hamid Ahamad, who ruled in this province in the time of Emperor Mahomed Toghalakh in A.H. 720, A.D. 1320.

1ـــ عمارت کرد این مسجد بعهد دولت سلطان
محمدشاه تغلقشاه که هست سلطان بن سلطان
بده والي این عرصر ملک تاج بن احمد
اما (ن) زانکو که از خونش دمیلرزند انس و جان
2ـــ کمینه بنده سلطان که نامش هست حمید احمد
بهفت صد بیست سن بوده است بذي القعده بنادان
خدا رحمت کند بر وي که این خواند دعاگوید
که یاربي بیامرزش که هست او از گناه کاران

This mosque was erected in the reign of Sultan Mahomed Shah Toglak Shah, Sultan, the son of Sultan. The master of this plain was Malek Tajoo bin Ahmed, protection from him whose terror makes men as well as the genii tremble (with fear) ! The mean slave of the Sultan, named Hamid Ahmed, be it known, made this in the month of Zilcad of the year 720* A.H. May God be kind to him who reads this and invokes this blessing. Oh God ! pardon him who is one of the sinners !

STONE INSCRIPTION IN THE OLD (MASJID) MOSQUE AT LOLIÂNÂ.
Dated A.H. 729.

Loliânâ, where this inscription was found, is a small village about miles from Walla or Valabhipur in Kâthiâvâḍ. The stone is a yellow sandstone, measuring 12″ × 8″ with four lines of Persian, of which some letters are lost. It mentions the building of the mosque in A.H. 729, A.D. 1329, by one Kar Mulla Shah.

1— بذات کرملا شاه بن محمد تعمیر نمود ه

2— بنده امیدوار برحمت پروردگار

3— خالق التخلق میدارد بعشرین ذی الحج سنر سبعمایه

4— بنا کرد این مسجد   ×   ×

Karmalâ Shah, son of Mahomed, himself built this.
The expectant slave hopes for the mercy of God, the Creator of the Universe. This mosque was built on the 20th of Zil-Haj 700 A.H.

STONE INSCRIPTION IN THE JUMÂ MASJID AT VERÂVALA IN KÂTHIÂVÂḌ.
Dated A.H. 732.

This inscription is engraved on a white marble slab, which measures 48″ × 10″. The stone is built up in one of the walls of the mosque and is very well-preserved. It is written partly in Persian and partly in Arabic. There are

---

*720 A.H. does not seem to be the proper date, because Juma Khan, who assumed the name of Sultan Mahomed, came to the throne in 725 A.H.

only two lines, in which it is said that the mosque was erected by Mahomed Najir, in the reign of Emperor Mahamad Shah, of Delhi. It is dated A.H. 732, A.D. 1331-32.

1 —— بسم الله الرحمن الرحيم   وان المساجد لله فلا تدعوامع الله احدا ٥ و قال النبي
علي الله عليه وسلم من بغي الله تعالي مسجداً بني الله له بيتاً في الجنة

2 —— عمارت اين مسجد خليفه قطب شاه بعد بادشاه محمد السلطان ابن السلطان
خلد الله ملكه السلطان با با خليفه × × بندۀ گناهكار اميد وار برحمت پروردگار صالح
سلطاني محمد نظير بني ما في التاريخ الغره رمضان سنر اثني و ثلثين وسبعمايه

In the name of God, the merciful and compassionate. " And verily the places of worship are set apart unto God : wherefore invoke not any other therein together with God."

And the prophet (may the blessing and peace of God be on him) said : " God will build a house for him in paradise who built a mosque for God the Most High."

This mosque of Khalife Kutb Shah was built by Baba Khalife Saleh Sultani Mahomed Nazir, the sinful slave expectant of the mercy of God, in the time of Mahomed Badshah, Sultan, the son of Sultan (may God perpetuate his kingdom). Dated 732 A.H.

STONE INSCRIPTION IN THE MOSQUE AT PRABHÂSA PÂṬANA.
Dated A.H. 770.

This inscription-stone is lying in the mosque called the mosque of Miṭhâshâ-bhang at Prabhâsa pâṭana, outside the town, near the great gate. This town is well known by its historical name of Samanâtha pâṭana on the south-west coast of Kâthiâvâḍ. The stone is a white sandstone with a surface measuring 19″ × 10″. There are five lines of a mixture of Persian and Arabic composition, of which one is written on the left side. Some of the letters have become quite indistinct. It mentions the erection of the mosque by the widow of a nobleman named Ismael bin Daud, in A.H. 770, A.D. 1368-69.

7

١ــ بسم الله الرحمٰن الرحيم   قال الله تعالي وان المساجد لله فلا

٢ــ تدعوا مع الله احدا ٥ قال النبي علي الله

٣ــ عليه وسلم من بغي مسجداً بني الله له قصراً في الجنة ٥ بنا كرد

٤ــ اين مسجد مسماة وارو بنت عبدالرحمان براي خداي تعالي درماه

ربيع الاخر سنه سبعين سبعمائة

٥ــ اين مسجد را بنا كرد بيوۀ امير اسماعيل بن امير داؤد شاه

In the name of God, the merciful and compassionate. God, the Most High,
said : " Verily the places of worship are set apart unto God : wherefore invoke not
any other therein together with God."

The Prophet (may the peace and blessing of God be on him) said : " God will
build a palace for him in paradise who built a mosque.

This mosque was built by (one named) Varu, daughter of *Abder Rehman*, for
God, the Most High, in the month of Rabi-ul-Akhar, 770 A.H.

This mosque was built by the widow of Amir Ismail, son of Amir Daud
Shah.

STONE INSCRIPTION IN THE IDA-GÂH NEAR MOSAMPURÂ AT GOGHÂ.

Dated A.H. 777.

The stone in which this inscription is cut is built up in the wall of the Idagáh,
in a suburb at the town of Goghâ, called Mosampurâ. It is a white stone
containing nine lines of mixed Persian and Arabic composition, of which several
letters are clear enough to make them out. It mentions the building of the Idagâh
by one Kamâl Hamid in the time of Zafar Khan in A.H. 777, A.D. 1375-76.

١ــ بسم الله الرحمن الرحيم

٢ــ واذ جعلنا البيت مثابة للناس وامنا فااتخذوا من مقام.ابراهيم مصلي

٣ــ در عيد (عهد) بناءاعظم شمس الدنيا و الدين نصرت بناء السلطان و بو قرخان

اعظم ظفرخان بن و جير الملك بنا كرده عمارت اين كارگاه بنده اميدوار

8

٤ ── برحمت پروردگار کمال حمید حرمین برانی بندا مومن رحمت کند که درین مقام برسد بندا امیدوار را بدعاء امان یاد کند

٥ ── بتاریخ پانزدهم ماه رجب (رجب وله) سنة سبع و سبعین و سبعمایة من هجرة النبی صلی الله علیه وسلم

In the name of God, the merciful and compassionate. And when we appointed the holy house of Mukkah to be a place of resort for mankind and a place of security, and said take the station of Abraham for a place of prayer.

In the time of the refuge of the great sun of the world and religion, the refuge of victory, the Sultan and the great Khan, viz., Zefer Khan, son of Vajih-ul-Mulk.

Kamal Hamid, pilgrim of Mecca and Medina, slave, hoping for the mercy of God, made this place of worship for the faithful.

May God bless him who comes here! May he remember the expectant slave with the blessing of safety.

Dated the 15th of Rajab, A.H. 777.

May the peace and blessing of God be on him.

STONE INSCRIPTION IN A MASJID NEAR THE GUNDI GATE AT GOGHÂ.

Dated A.H. 780.

This stone is raised near the mosque built near the house of one Dâdâ Mulla on the way leading to the Gundi Gate at Goghâ. It is a hard black stone with a face measuring 17" × 14". The inscription appears to have been in Persian, as, with the exception of a few words, the whole of it has become undecipherable. There are in all nine lines. It is dated A.H. 780, A.D. 1378-79.

(هو العدل)

١ ── بادشاه مظفر بود نور بار جهان   مرد افغان یکي خان اعظم المکان
٢ ── عمارتي نباشد اینسان نوادر دربے نوسنگ اگر بم بگردد در نقصان دردان در نشان

9

3ـــ بهر آن تاریخ کرد × (ربیع الثانی × بفال شد یاد) در عالم قلم زیل

4ـــ × × × × × × × ازیک آذرا نیابند و زان حال در منزل
گمان

5ـــ × × × × × دارد عدم میزان بناشدی (وز) عد نشان

6ـــ × × (بنیادش) (شد) × (ارقام آخرش باد پنهان)

7ـــ × × × × × × × ، × الی کریم ذیشان

8ـــ × این × بشکند × × × × (برین گنبذ ×

9ـــ نویسد × در × ، × × × هفصد هشتاد شد ×

As many of the letters cannot be deciphered it is difficult to find out what it contains. The word "Muzeffer" can be read, but it is doubtful.

In the same line a name is distinctly read, which is Khan Ânaj Mulamakan, A.H. 780.

STONE INSCRIPTION IN THE RAHEMAT MASJID AT MÂNGROL.
Dated A.H. 784.

This inscription is cut into a yellow stone and is built up in the wall of the Rahemat *masjid* situated to the north outside the town of Mângrol in Kâthiâvâd. Its outer surface containing the inscription measures 36″ × 21″ and has seven lines of Arabic arranged as follows :—The first line is in the middle, then two on each side, then there is one line at the top and one at the bottom. It mentions the building of a mosque called Rahemat in the time of Sultan Fîroz Shah of Delhi in A.H. 784, A.D. 1382-83.

یا الله   یا الله   یا الله

1ـــ قال الله تعالی و ان المساجد لله فلا تدعوا مع الله احدا

2ـــ قال الله تعالی انما یعمر مساجد الله من آمن بالله و الیوم الاخر واقام الصلوة
و آتی الزکوة و لم یخش الا الله نعسی اولئک من المبتدین

3ـــ قال علیه السلام الدَّنیا داحَّة لیس فیها راحة

3

٤ — قال عليه السلام الدّنيا ساعةٌ فاجعلها طاعةً

٥ — قال عليه السلام من بني الله مسجّدًا بني الله له في الجنة قصرًا
بناكرد اين مسجد رحمت افضل القضاة صاحب التخير والتحسنات فاضي
القطب باسم سيد السّادات شيخ المشايخ قطب الاوليا جلال الحق والشرع
والدين   .

٦ — در عهد سلطان الاعظم المعظم مالك الجود والكرم الواثق بتائيد الرحمن
ابو المظفر فيروز شاه سلطان خلد الله ملكه
بتاريخ ×   شهر ×   سنة اربع وثمانين وسبعمائه

God, the Most High, said : " Verily the places of worship are set apart unto
God : wherefore invoke not any other therein together with God."

But he only shall visit the temples of God who believeth in God and the last
day, and is constant at prayer, and payeth the legal alms, and feareth God alone.
These perhaps may become of the number of those who are rightly directed.

The Prophet (may the peace of God be on him!) said : " The world is a
pageant ; and there is no repose there."

The Prophet (may the peace of God be on him !) said : " The world is transitory, therefore pray there."

The Prophet (may the peace of God be on him!) said : " He who built a
mosque for God will have a palace built for him in paradise by God.

This " Mosque of Mercy " (musjid-e-rahemat) was built by the greatest of the
Kazis, the doer of good and meritorious acts, Kazi-ul-Kutb in the name of the
best Sayed (descendant of Mahomed), the greatest of the great, the pole-star of the
friends of God, the glory of truth, and the sacred law and religion.

In the reign of Sultan Firozshah (may God perpetuate his rule!) the greatest and honoured Sultan, the possessor of liberality and generosity ; confident of
the help of God and the father of victory.

*   * Month 784 A.H.

STONE INSCRIPTION IN THE MOSQUE OF THE BORÂHS NEAR THE BUNDER GATE AT MÂNGROL.

Dated A.H. 785.

This inscription-stone is built up in the side-wall of the Borâh's mosque at Mângrol. It is a slab of white marble well preserved, with a face measuring 21″ × 18″. It is written partly in Arabic and partly in Persian, of which there are in all ten lines. It says that the mosque was caused to be built by Iz-ud-din bin Aramshah in the reign of Emperor Fîroz Shah in A.H. 785, A.D. 1383-84.

———

١ ــ بسم الله الرحمن الرحيم

٢ ــ قال الله تبارك وتعالي و ان المساجد لله فلا تدعوا مع الله احدا

٣ ــ در عهد خسروبي كه شهان پيش دركبش سر بر زمين نهادد چون خاكند در روهش

٤ ــ فيروز شاه شاه جهان گير ودين پناه   بنياد كفر زو شده اندر گل تباه

٥ ــ نور چراغ شرع ازو يافته فيا   در عهد دولتش كه مبادانش انزرا

٦ ــ بنياد اين مقام شد از فضل كردگار   ازسعي عزالدين بن ارامشه بكار

٧ ــ اتمام هم بدولت عهدش شد اين مقام   اميدش آنكه عفو گناهش بود تمام

٨ ــ از سال هجرت نيوي بود هفتصد   هشتاد و پنج گشته بروز آيد از عدد

٩ ــ يارب زفضل و عون خويش عفو كن تمام   با نيش را گناه بكونين والسلام

١٠ ــ بخط العبد الضعيف الراجي الي رحمة الله تعالي طاهر عثمان جعفري

In the name of God, the Merciful and Compassionate. God the Blessed and the High said: "Verily the places of worship are set apart unto God: wherefore invoke not any other therein together with God."

(1) In the reign of the king, before whose court princes lie prostrated like dust in his way. (2) Firozshah, the world-conquering king, the protector of the faith, the foundation of infidelity (*kufra*) was destroyed in the dust by him.

The light of the lamp of religion (*sharè*) became brilliant through him. May it not fade away during his time.

By the endeavour of Iz-ud-din, son of Aramshah, the foundation of this building was laid, through the grace of God.

The building was completed also in the same reign; his hope was that all his sins may be pardoned.

According to calculation it was 785 A.H. Oh God! Forgive through thy grace and help the sins of the builder in both the worlds! and peace.

This is written by Taher Osman Jaferi, the mean slave expectant of the mercy of the Most High.

STONE INSCRIPTION IN THE MOSQUE NEAR THE JAIL-GATE INSIDE THE TOWN OF MÂNGROL.

Dated A.H. 787.

This inscription is placed in the mosque which is near the Jail-gate at Mângrol. The stone is of white marble, having its outer surface of 27″ × 19″. The inscription is contained in eighteen lines of Arabic and Persian, of which two lines on its two sides have become so indistinct that it is difficult to decipher them. It mentions the building of the mosque by Saïd Mahomed Khwaja in the time of Emperor Fîroz Shah, whose vazir he was. The year given therein is A.H. 787, A.D. 1385.

---

1 — و ان المساجد لله فلا تدعوا مع الله احدا بناء (مسجد محمد خواجر
فريد الدين كلان يكي از × × × الشيخ نصير الدين محمود كبائي چشتيان بنائي مسجد
محمد خواجر عطار حضرت × × ملك × × × × × × × ×
× × × × بدعا ياد نمايد × × × ×

ستاده بردرش انعام خواهان	2 — بعهد دولت شاهي كه شاهان
نداند ظلم را كس نام و نشان	3 — شهر فيروز كاندر داد و عدلش
بذات مشهر و صف سليمان	4 — اميد دولتش جن و بشر را
نديده كس بدهر از نسل انسان	5 — جهانداري چنين و هم جهانگير
بگيتي تا مهر و مهر مت تابان	6 — خدايا داريش دايم سلامت
بميمون ساعت و اكرام سبحان	7 — بنا اين مبارك مسجد نو
محمد خواجهٔ از بود علي كان	8 — بسمي دولت صدر الاكابر
عطاي خو (ع) او بيرون امكان	9 — بذاتش فضل و بذل ازحد بيرون
بهركس در جهان او كرده احسان	10 — صفا و لطف او بيرون مقدار
و زير مملكت شايد بسلطان	11 — زاوصاف كمالش خود چه گويم
فزوده دفت ديگر بر سر آن	12 — ز هفتصد بود تاريخبخش بيشتاد
خدا با نيش را بتخشد حق آن	13 — باتمام آمد اين فرخنده بنياد
نعيم خلد بتخشادش فراوان	14 — بدار بي فنا و بي نهايت
سلامت داردش از كيد نقضان	15 — بعالم ياد شد روز قيامت
خدا گرداندش مقرون بايمان	16 — دعا كردم من و آمين ملك گفت

Verily the places of worship are set apart unto God : wherefore invoke not any other therein together with God.

The builder of the mosque, Mahomed Khajeh *Farid-ud-din* (Kalan ?), one of the * * * Sheekh Nasir-ud-din Mahomed Kabai Chishtian.

The building of the mosque of Mahomed Khajeh Attar, honoured by the exalted Creator * * *

In the time of the reign of the king, at whose doors other kings stand expecting gifts ; Firoz Shah, under whose justice and equity nobody knows any trace of oppression ; man as well as genii hope to be benefited by his wealth; himself illustrious with virtues such as Solomon had ; such a ruler and conqueror nobody has ever seen born of man ; Oh God ! keep him always safe in this world as long as the sun and the moon are shining; the construction of this blessed new mosque began in an auspicious hour and with the liberality of God ; with the help of the fortune of Mahomed Khajeh, the chief of the great ones, and a descendant of Ali ; his kindness and generosity have no bounds ; the munificence of his nature being beyond the bounds of possibility ; his purity and his benevolence being beyond estimation ; he has laid everybody in this world under obligation ; how can I describe the perfection of his virtues ? (he) is a minister of the kingdom, fit for the Sultan ; the date of the completion of this blessed building was seven hundred and eighty, plus seven ; may God give the builder his due ! May God give him innumerable delights of Paradise in the imperishable and endless world ! (its) memory is preserved in this world to the day of resurrection ; may God keep him free from injurious deceits ! I invoked this blessing and the angel said '*amen.*' May God fasten him to the faith !

STONE INSCRIPTION OF THE DARGAH NEAR THE RÂVALI MASJID AT MÀNGROL.

Dated A.H. 788.

This inscription is cut into a soft yellow stone built up in the wall of a *Dargah* near the Râvali Masjid at Mângrol. The face of the stone measures 25″ × 19″ with twelve lines of Persian mixed with Arabic. It has crumbled down in some places. It mentions that a mosque was caused to be built by a nobleman, Malik Abdul Malik, in the reign of Emperor Firozshah in A.H. 788, A. D. 1386.

4

۱ — بسم الله الرحمن الرحيم

۲ — قال الله تبارك وتعالي وأن المساجد لله فلا تدعوا مع الله احدا

۳ — قال النبي صلي الله عليه وسلم من بني الله مسجداً بن الله له في الجنة قصراً

۴ — بعهد دولت فيروز شاهي ۞ كه حكمش در گرفت از ماه و ماهي

۵ — سكندر دولتي دريا سپاهي ۞ فريدون حشمتي گردون كلاهي

۶ — نسيم از خلق او صد بهره گيرد ۞ زلال از لطف او صد جان پذيرد

۷ — ز خوانش ريزه چيني حاتم طي ۞ ز درگاهش نقيبي خسرو كي

۸ — بسعي همت ماخدوم زاده ۞ كه هست او در سخا ابري كشاده

۹ — ز قلماتش كه نيساني شده مست ۞ ملك عبدالملك پور حسامست

۱۰ — × × رفت × بنامش ۞ كه بادا در بقا (عهدي) تماهش

۱۱ — (بهشت) در شمار (هست) از عدن ۞ بهشتاد (خوانند) شد بفتصد

۱۲ — خدا يش اجر اين بتخشد بدارين ۞ گناهش عفو كن از وي بكونين

---

1. In the name of the merciful and compassionate God.

2. God, the blessed and the exalted, said: "Verily the places of worship are set apart unto God: wherefore invoke not any other therein together with God."

3. Said the Prophet: "May God look with favour on him and His peace be on him! God will build a palace in paradise for him *who builds* a mosque for God."

4. In the reign of Firozshah, whose command had effect over the moon and the fish.

5. Whose fortune is like that of Alexander, whose army is as innumerable as (the waves of) the sea; whose splendour is like that of Faridun, and whose crown is like the dome of sky.

6. The morning breeze derives a hundred advantages from his disposition; the pure water is endowed with a hundred lives from his generosity.

7. Hatim Tai might pick crumbs at his table; and Kai Khosro might stand sentinel at his court.

8. By the effort of the magnanimity of the nobleman who is like the rain-bespattering cloud in liberality.

9. The strokes of whose pen have made the (pearl-producing) rain-drops of spring wanton; (such) is Malck Abdul Malek, son of Hisam.

10. *　*　*　*　may his age end in eternity!

11. The number (of the year) 788 is arrived at by calculation.

12. May God give him the reward of this in both the worlds! pardon his sins in either existence!

STONE INSCRIPTION OF THE MOSQUE OF AHAMAD JAMÂDÂR AT MÂNGROL.

Dated A.H. 791.

The mosque of Ahamad Jamâdâr in which this inscription-stone is found is outside the town of Mângrol and to the east of it. The inscription is cut into a slab of white marble with a surface of 20″ × 14″ and is well preserved. It contains seventeen lines of mixed Persian and Arabic composition, and mentions the raising of a mausoleum over the remains of a martyr named Malik Ahamad by his son Iliâs with a direction to read the Koran there. It gives the date A.H. 791, A.D. 1388.

---

1 — بسم الله الرحمن الرحيم انا لله و انا اليه راجعون

2 — سرشت آدمي چون هست از خاك   رجوعش باز شد بر خاك نمناك

3 — اميران و ملوك و خان و شاهان   تباپوشان هريك كو كلاهان

4 — خصوص اين مرد صاحب قبر دين دار   كه از دنياء فاني رفت هشيار

5 — ملك والاء احمد ترك غازي   كه كرده در غزا بر ترك تازي

6 — بشهر نغر نيكو داشت جائي   ز اجداد و ز آبايش سرائي

7 — كنون سر در نقاب خاك كرده   لباس زندكاني چاك كرده

8 — مريد قطب ركن الشرع و الدين   سهروردي كه بود اقطاب در دين

9 — جوار رحمت حق باد جانش   بيامرزد ز فضل خود خدايش

10 — ز هجرت بود هفتصد يك نود سال   كه راحت كرد زين دنياء ذوالحال

11 — ربيع اول از مه بيست و پنجم   تواريخبخش بتاب ماه و انجم

12 — كه جانش را بعليين بردند   تن خاكي بدين جايش سپردند

13 — نود سالش بنائي عمر بودست   خدا را بس پرستشها نمود است

14 — بجائي خود خلف الياس بگذاشت   بسا ملك جهانرا ديد در گشت   كوايف تا كه مرقوم نلم گشت

15 — بناء مقبره و ختم قرآن   كه پاس او جملۀ بند بدرداشت

16 — هرانكو فاتحه خواند باخلاص   هدايت يافت از توفيق يزدان

17 — بيامرزد خدا از فضل و اكرام   رسد بر تربت اين بندۀ خاص   برآرد روز حشر با كام انجام

In the name of God, the merciful and compassionate :

We are God's and unto Him shall we surely return.

Since man is created out of dust, to moist earth he returned.

Lords, khans, kings, and emperors, (as well as) those who put on robes and every one who wears curved hats (they all return to dust). Especially the religious man who is interred here went away from the transitory world briskly. (His name) Malik Vala Ahmed, a crusader, who undertook great many plundering expeditions in war in the cause of religion. He was a native of the good city of Nagz, where his ancestors had their mansion.

Now he has hid his face behind the veil of earth, having torn off the garb of life. (He was) a disciple of Sohr Vardi, who was the pole-star of religion.

May his place be beside the mercy of God! May God forgive him through His generosity! He departed from this world * * in 791 A.H. His date, by the revolution of the moon and stars, was the 25th of the Rabi-ul-avval. His soul was carried to heaven while his earthly body was deposited here.

His age was 90 years, and he worshipped God always ; he had travelled over many countries of the world * * which has been written.

He left a son Aliâs behind him, who guarded all the counsels of his father. Through the grace of God he got the right direction to build the tomb and read the Koran.

He who approaches the grave of this chosen slave shall read the chapters of Koran, *viz.* (Fatieh and Akhlas).

God may pardon him through His generosity and kindness ! and may fulfil on the day of resurrection his final desire.

STONE INSCRIPTION OF THE GÂDI GATE AT MÂNGROL.

Dated A.H. 805.

Near the Gâdi's Gate at Mângrol and to the west of it there is a *chopâta.** In its left side-wall this piece of white marble is built up. On its outer surface it measures 24" × 24", and has twelve lines of Persian, wherein it is said that the town-wall of Mângrol was caused to be built by Malik Musa, Kotwal of Sorath and a brother of Malik Yâkub, Governor of the Province. It is also said that the Governor of Gujarât at the time was Zafar Khan. It is dated A.H. 805, A. D. 1402-03.

---

* A small square room attached to the gate.

کرشد خلقت از وی نمایان سماک	۱ — بعون عنایات غفار پاک
سما را معلّق ورق بر ورق	زمین را نهاده طبّا تا طبق
بناء کرم تا کرم بنیاد کرد	۲ — جهان بود بیران رانر آباد کرد
ز ذاتش کر ذات جهان را قبول	محمد فرستاد بر ما رسول
شده نصرتش یار و بختت بلند	۳ — بدوران عهد شر زورمند
کر من من سرش شد سزا بارگاه	شهنشاه نصرت جهان بادشاه
بدست تمامش نر پا بر سریر .	۴ — مظفر ظفرخان اعظم وزیر
جهان دیده مردان صاحب سخن	چنین گفت پیشینگان کبس
نبود و نباشد جهان داوری	۵ — کر در عرصۀ گوجرات چنین آمری
براند التیشم رعیت نواز	بهر سو ازو آمری سرفراز
ز پاکی ذاتش شرف بر ملک	۶ — ز جاه و ز عزت قدم بر فلک
کر سورتیمر بفرماندهی شاد کام	ملک والی عهد یعقوب نام
ملک ببر سپهر سیر گردون و تار	۷ — تمیم احمد بود یل نامدار
باحسان احسن کر توفیق باد	بتوفیق ایزد بنا نو نهاد
کر سد سکندر بود شرمسار	۸ — بمنگلور حصنیست سنگین حصار
نر حصنی بران زینتی و زیب او	فلک را رازیست باشیب او
زبیواد کرده ملک سربسر	۹ — نبد بستر ز آهن حلیقا ء د ر
زرنایایش در آهن گرفت	بهر تختمر آهن دو صد زر گرفت
ملک موسی کوتوال دیار	۱۰ — برادر بدش کار کار فرماء کار
بساند کر تا نام و نیشان او	کر این نقش بستر بفرمان او
ز ماه رجب چهارده شد تمام	۱۱ — بتاریخ یفتصد نود یفتت تام
چنین نقش پیدا شده بینظیر	باسناد قاضی و ملک ظهیر
دید فاتحر مرحبایش کند	۱۲ — هر انکو بخواند دعایش کند

With the help of the favours of the holy Giver, from whom the people of the world came to see the sky:

He has created the earth, placing one stratum over another like plate over plate; and the skies suspended like leaf over leaf:

5

The world was barren, (He) made it prosperous. So that He laid the foundation of benevolence.

Mahomed was sent as prophet to us, who was such that the world accepted him.

In the time of the powerful king, victorious and fortunate ;

The emperor of victory, the king of the world ;

He whose head became worthy of Government.

Muzefer Zefer Khan, the great Vazeer, with whose absolute help you place your foot on the throne ;

Ancient writers, experienced people, masters of words, have said this :

That in the length and breadth of Gujerat no Governor like this has been or will be.

In every direction every Amir is held in high honour owing to him ; the surname of the king came to be " The bestower on the subjects. "

His splendour and respect raise him to the skies ; in personal piety he is superior to the angel. The name of the Governor of the age, Malik Yákub, who bore sway over Soreth happily. Zamim Ahmed, the famous hero, was a Malik like a tiger, soldier-like and as exalted in honour as the skies.

By the grace of God he laid a new foundation ; for noble gratitude like this may the grace of God befall him !

There is such a strong stone fortress in Manglore (Mângrol) that the Wall of Alexander feels humiliated before it.

The depth of the fortress is in secret communication with the sky ; there is no other fortress like it in splendour and pomp.

The rings of the gate are not made of iron, but the Malik made them all of steel.

Every piece of iron cost two hundred gold coins ; gold gave its deputyship to iron. His brother was the chief officer, viz., Malik Musa, the Kotwal of the district. This structure was made at his (Zamim Ahmed's) command by him (Musa), so that the name and fame of the former may last as long as the fortress.

This was completed on the 14th Rajab, A.H. 797.

Such unequalled composition came into being with the authority of the Kazi as well as Malik Zahir.

Every one who reads this should bless him ; read the chapter of the Koran and praise him.

STONE INSCRIPTION OF THE GÂDI GATE AT MÂNGROL.

Dated A.H. 805.

This inscription is in the same place as the preceding one and appears to have been placed there along with it in the same year. It is also cut into a white marble slab, a little smaller than its companion, being 18″ × 12″. It contains eight lines in Persian to the effect that the kotwals of Mângrol are prohibited from levying the tax on marriages of the Hindus and Ahiras. This order was promulgated by Malek Yatim-ul-lah, the then Governor of Sorath. It is dated A.H. 805, A.D. 1402-03.

---

١ ـــ يا اللهُ الله معين الضعفا بسم الله الرحمن الرحيم

٢ ـــ درسال شهور منه خمس ثمانمايۀ بندۀ ملك العالي

٣ ـــ معين الدوله والدين ملك ملكشه بدر

٤ ـــ يتيم الله معاليه مقطع سورتّهه براي آباداني

٥ ـــ قصبه منگلور و فراغ خاطر خلق هر وجهي كه بوقت

٦ ـــ تزويج هندوان و اهيران كوتوال قصبه مذكور مي

٧ ـــ ستاند دور كرده وگذاشته بعد ازين نستانند وغيره همچنين

٨ ـــ بر خلق مذكور معاف دارند تا نجات ديني و دنياوي باشد

Oh God! God! the Helper of the weak.

In the name of God, the merciful and compassionate: During the months of the years 805, *Malek Malekshah Bedr Yatim-ul-lah*, the grandee of the territory of Sorath, and the servant of the exalted king, the defender of the kingdom and the faith, abolished and remitted for the sake of the prosperity of the town of Mângrol, and for the contentment of the minds of the people, every kind of impost which the *kotewal* of the said town used to levy on the occasions of marriages of the Hindus and the Ahiran henceforth it was not to be levied; and that the inhabitants of the said town be also excused from paying such other imposts in order that there may be spiritual and temporal freedom.

STONE INSCRIPTION OF THE MASJID NEAR THE MOṬÁ DAR-VÁZÁ AT PÁṬAṆA.

Dated A.H. 820.

The *masjid* in which this inscription is found is at present known as that of Jamádár Mahomad's mosque. It is near the *Moṭá Darvázá*, or the great gate, at Páṭaṇa, a small town under the Junágaḍh State, and where there is the celebrated temple of Somanáth. The outer surface of the stone, which is a common white sand-stone, measures 22″ × 14″, and contains five lines of mixed Arabic and Persian composition. The two lines at the top have become too indistinct to decipher. It mentions that the mosque was caused to be built by one Faz-lul-lah (Faz-ul-lah) when Sultan Ahamadshah was ruling over Gujarát in the year A.H. 820, A.D. 1417-18.

١—بسم الله الرحمن الرحيم

٢—وان المساجد لله فلا تدعوا مع الله احدا

٣—بتاريخ بيست و پفتم ماه رمضان شريف عشرين و ثمانمايه در عهد سلطان احمد بن

٤—محمد بن مظفر شاه سلطان بناكنانيده فضل الله احمد

٥—ابو رمجا هركه بخواند بنده را بدعاء ايمان و فاتحه ياد كند

تمت

In the name of God, the merciful and compassionate : " Verily the places of worship are set apart unto God : wherefore invoke not any other therein together with God."

On the 27th day of the month of Ramzani Sheriff, A.H. 820, in the reign of Sultan Ahmed bin Mahamed bin Muzzefer Shah Sultan, Faz-lul-lah Ahmed Abu Remja caused this to be made. May he who reads this remember (me) the slave with the blessing of faith and the repetition of the first chapter of the Koran !

STONE INSCRIPTION IN THE GRAVEYARD NEAR THE GÂDI GATE AT MÂNGROL.

Dated A.H. 820.

This stone is raised on the *chotrá** in the graveyard near the Gâdi Gate at Mângrol on the Kâthiâvâd Coast. The face of the stone measures 24″ × 13″, and contains four lines of Persian with almost all the letters broken. It mentions the building of a mosque by one Shah Alum in the year A.H. 820, A.D. 1417-18, during the reign of Sultan Ahamad Shah of Gujarât.

1ــعمارات اين مسجد وباغنجات در عهد قطب ملک شاه عالم بادشاه
نا صرالدنيا والدين ابوالفتح احمد شاه بن محمد شاه بن مظفر شاه السلطان

2ــبانی(عالم) × (شده) ملک الشرق ملک گجرات × × (الراجی)
الی الله (لحمد) ×

3ـ × × × × × × × در ماه محرم شهر سنه سته وعشرين
وثمانمايه (ازٔ) (قرض)

4ـ(حسنه) بنا (کرد اين) امير قطب عالم عمارات × × × × ×
× ×

This mosque, with its pretty gardens, was made in the reign of Ahmedshah, son of Mahomed, son of Muzeffer Shah, Sultan, son of Sultan, the polestar of the kingdom, the emperor of the world, the defender of the faith and the world, father of victory.

    *   *   *   *   *   *

In the month of Mohurrum A.H. 820 this was constructed by Amir Kutbe Alum.

---

* A square open and detached stone verandah (?)

6

STONE INSCRIPTION IN A MOSQUE NEAR MAHUVÂ.

Dated A.H. 826.

The mosque in which this inscription is, is near the small town of Mahuvâ, on the way to Talagâjarâdâ, a small village to the·north of it. It is cut into a white marble slab and is well preserved. There are only two lines of Persian on a surface measuring 34″ × 12″. It mentions that one Malik Asare-Mulk erected the mosque in the reign of Sultan Ahamadshah of Gujarât. The date of the inscription is A.H. 826, A.D. 1422-23.

———

١ـــبسم الله الرحمن الرحيم وان المساجد لله فلا تدعوا مع الله احدا من
بناء الدنيا بيتاً بني الله في الاخرة

٢ـــدرتلافي نياز اين كارگاه درعهد سلطان احمد خلدالله ملكه اما اين حقير
مُلِكُ آثارِ مُلكُ وجوهر تاريخ ششم شعبان في سنه ثمانمائة ستة و عشرين
سلطان العهد وشان ملتين

———

A

In the name of the merciful and compassionate God : " Verily the places of worship are set apart unto God : wherefore invoke not any other therein together with God ; God will build a (house for him) in the next world who built a house for God in this world.

B

By way of making amends for this post ; in the reign of Sultan Ahmed, may God perpetuate his kingdom, this insignificant Malik *Asaré-Mulk* (or and) *Javehr* :— 6th day of the month of Shaban in the year 826 :—the Sultan of the time and the dignity of the two communities (Mahomedans and Hindus ?).

STONE INSCRIPTION OF A MASJID NEAR THE FOUZDAR'S RESIDENCE AT VERÂVAL.

Dated A.H. 834.

The musjid in which this inscription is placed is near the residence of the police officer of the district of Verâval under Junâgadh on the south-west coast. It is cut into a white marble slab measuring 45″ × 7″, and contains three lines in Persian mixed with Arabic. The letters have become very indistinct. It is dated A.H. 834, A.D. 1430-31, when the throne of Gujarât was occupied by king Ahamad Shah.

بسم الله الرحمن الرحيم و ان المساجد لله فلاتدعوامع الله احدا درعهد سلطان

اعظم ناصرالدنيا و الدين ابوالنصر سلطان (احمد) بن محمد شاه بن مظفر شاه (×) سلطان

بنا كرد عمارت اين مسجد برادر محمد شاه بن سلطان مظفرشاه خلد الله ملكه وسلطنت،

و اين ملك حسين مظفر حسيني ثم ذالك منه اربع ثلاثين ثمانماية شهر ربيع الثاني × × ×

In the name of God, the merciful and compassionate :—Verily, the places of worship are set apart unto God : wherefore invoke not any other therein together with God. This mosque was built by (Malik Husain Muzeffer *Hassani*) the brother of Mahomed Shah, son of Sultan Muzeffer Shah (may God perpetuate his kingdom and his rule !).

In the reign of Sultan Ahmed, the greatest, the honoured, the defender of the world and the faith, the father of victory, son of Mahomed Shah, son of Muzeffer Shah Sultan. And after this A.H. 834, the month of Rabi-us-Sani. * * *

STONE INSCRIPTION NEAR THE (MHOṬÂ) GRAND GATE AT PÂṬAṆA.

Dated A.H. 836.

This stone is lying loose near the *Mhotâ Darvâzâ*, or the grand gate at Pâṭaṇa, near Verâval, under Junâgaḍh, on the south-west coast of Kâthiâvâd. It measures on its surface 19″ × 10″ and contains five lines of Persian, the letters of which have become very indistinct. The inscription mentions the erection of some building in the year A.H. 836, A.D. 1432-33, in the time of Firozshah * * of Ahamadshah of Gujarât.

1ـ برائي خشنودي و رضاء خالق الصمد فيروز شاه بن   ×   بادشاه احمد شاه

2ـ بن محمد شاه بن مظفرشاه سلطان خلدالله ملکه وسلطنته   ×   ×   شده بود

3ـ حضرت شاه (ابن) جناب   ×   ×   (امرشد براي درگهش   ×   مي شدند هر که بیاید بد عائي)

4ـ (بدي دست نزده مزاحمت ندهد بامرے خطا و بي فرمان نکرده باشد مجرم خواهد)

5ـ بود و ذالک في التاسع من ذي القعد سنه ستر ثلثين و ثمانمایه

For the delight and pleasure of the sublime Creator.

Firozshah * * Ahmedshah, son of Mahomedshah, son of Sultan Muzeffer Shah. May God perpetuate his kingdom and rule!

*   *   *   *   *   *

No visitor should give trouble by his imprecation, otherwise he will have committed a fault and disobedience, (and)

He will be a sinner.

This was made on the 9th of Zilead A.H. 836.

STONE INSCRIPTION IN THE CHÂNDANI MASJID AT PÂTANÂ.

Dated A.H. 866.

This inscription is cut into a slab of white marble placed in the Chândani Masjid at Pâtanâ, also called Prabhâs Pâtanâ under Junâgadh. It is an oblong piece with a surface measuring 27″ × 8″ and contains three lines of Persian with a sprinkling of Arabic words. It mentions that in A.H. 866, A.D. 1461-62, the mosque was caused to be built by one Nas-ul-lah during the reign of Ahamadshah II. * of Gujarât.

_____

١ـــقال الله تعالي وان المساجد لله فلاتد عوا مع الله احدا قال النبي صلي الله
عليه و سلم من بناء مسجدًا بني الله تعالي في الجنة قصرا

٢ـــعمارت اين مسجد همايون بعهد شاه اعاظم المعظم الوائق بتائيد الرحمن قطب
الدنيا والدين ابو المظفر احمد شاه بن محمد شاه بن احمد شاه بن محمد
شاه بن مظفرشاه السلطان خلد الله ملكه و سلطانه بنده ضعيف النحيف الراجي
الي رحمت الله الحنان المنان شمس بن صدر بن شمس بن ×

٣ـــالقريشي اللحي المعروف بملك بده گره و (از) سعي اوكار اين مسجد تمام
كرد بنده اميدوار برحمت پروردگار صدر بن شمس درکه درين مسجد نماز
بگذارد بدعاء خير وثبات دلي اين گذاهكاران باني سازنده مسجد را ياد
مي آرند تا موجب ثواب دائمي دردوجهاني گردد بتاريخ دهدهم ماه رجب
مرجب شهور سنه ست وستين وثمانماية قدره أضعف العباد نصرالله بن ابراهيم
بن شمر بن محمد لما يذكر

_____

'God, the Most High, said : " Verily, the places of worship are set apart unto God : wherefore invoke not any other therein together with God." The Prophet, may the blessing and peace of God be on him, said : " God will build a palace for him who built a mosque for God."

This blessed mosque was built in the time of Ahmedshah, the greatest of the great kings, the firm, God-aided, the pole star of the world, and the faith, the father of victory. May God perpetuate his kingdom and his rule! (He was) the

_____

* The reigning Sultan of Gujarât at the time was Mahumud Bigra and not Ahamadshah II.

7

son of Mahomed Shah, son of Ahmed Shah, son of Mahomed Shah, son of Muzeffer Shah, the Sultan.

And this mosque was finished by Sadr, son of Shams, the slave, expecting the mercy of God, through the endeavour of Shams, son of Sadr, son of Shams, at Koreish-al-lahiya *alias* Malek Budeh Gareh. The humble and weak slave expecting the kindness of God, the most affectionate and beneficent. May those who offer prayers in this mosque remember the sinful builders of this mosque with the blessing of welfare and firmness of heart ; so that they may become the cause of eternal merit in the two worlds.

Dated 17th Rajabi-mur-rajab A.H. 866. May God honour Nasr-ul-lah, the most humble slave, son of Ibrahim, son of Omar, son of Mahomed, when this is remembered !

STONE INSCRIPTION IN A MOSQUE NEAR THE CUSTOMS HOUSE AT VERÂVAL.

Dated A.II. 870.

The mosque where this inscription is found is situated near the *Mândavi* or the Customs House at Verâval under Junâgadh on the south-west coast. It is cut into a white marble slab with a surface of 46″ × 17″ in three lines of Arabic. It says that in A.H. 870, A.D. 1465-66, Mahmud Shah II. of Gujarât caused this mosque to be built in honour of one Mahomed.

---

1 ــ بسم الله الرحمن الرحيم وان المساجد لله فلا تدعوا مع الله احدا × × × × × × × × × × × وقال النبي صلي الله عليه وسلم × × × ×

2 ــ × × × قد بني هذا المسجد قدوة الشريف عمدة المشايخ عاشرت الامن السلطان الاعظم مالك الرقاب ابوالفتح محمود شاه بن محمد شاه بن احمد شاه ابن محمد شاه بن

3 ــ مظفر السلطان خلد الله ملكه وامره وذلك بنص كالذخائر العلية محمد بن حاجي علي بن محمد الكيلاني فرحمه الله من النار في تاريخ عاشر شهر ربيع الاخر سنه سبعين وثمانمايته

In the name of God, the merciful and compassionate : " And verily the places of worship are set apart for God : wherefore invoke not any other therein together with God."   *   *   *

And the Prophet (may the peace and blessing of God be on him !) said : * * * *

This mosque was built by Mahomudshah, son of Mahomedshah, son of Ahmedshah, son of Mahomedshah, son of Sultan Muzeffer, the honour of the nobleman, the support of the wise, the augmenter of security, the greatest Sultan, the master of necks, and the father of victory ; may God perpetuate his kingdom and his rule.

For raising the fame of Mahomed, son of Haji Ali, son of Mahomed Gilani, (who is) like a treasure of sublimity ! May God mercifully keep him away from hell ! The 10th of Rabi-ul-Akber, 870 A.H.

STONE INSCRIPTION IN THE JUMA MASJID AT DVÂRIKA.

Dated A.H. 877.

The Juma *Masjid* in which this inscription stone is placed is called the Hâji Karamânis *Masjid*. It is at Dvârika, the ancient and celebrated capital of Krishna, now a possession of the Gâekvâd of Barodâ, in Kâthiâwâd. On a surface of 19″ × 13″ there are six lines in Persian, of which the fifth line has lost several letters. The year given appears to be A.H. 877, A.D. 1472, though the first figure of hundreds is not clear enough. It is said that the great mosque was built by Sultan Mahmûd Bigharâ, when he made the conquest of Saukhadhâr off the Jagat point.

از فضل حق سبحانه و تعالی عمارت این مسجد جامع درعهد (محمود) شاه
اعظم ابو المظفر (فیروز الدنیا والدین) خان (معز الاسلام) و المسلمین ملک
المعزز شمس الملک (بنا شد) × × × × در ماه ربیع الاول سنه
سبع وسبعین و(ثما نمایة)

Through the grace of God, the most holy and most high, this great mosque was constructed in the time of Mahmûd Shah, the great lord, the father of victory, the prosperity of the world and the religion ; honoured by Islam and the Mahomedans ; the respected king ; the sun of the country.

In the month of Rabi-ul-awwal (8)77, A.H. 877.

28

STONE INSCRIPTION IN THE NEW MASJID OF THE KÂJIS AT PÂTANA.

*Dated A.H. 9 * **

This inscription is engraved on a piece of black granite and is one of the two inscriptions that are found in the same *masjid*, known as the Kaji's mosque at Pátana on the south-west coast of Káthiáwád, under Junágadh. It measures 25″ × 17″ on its surface and contains twenty-eight lines of Arabic. The inscription mentions the conquest and capture of the town with the celebrated shrine of Somanáth by Sultan Mahmúd Bigarha. The year cannot be clearly made out as the first figure, viz., that of hundred, can only be deciphered. Still it can be said from the years in which Mahmúd Bigarha led his armies into Sorath that it must be A.H. 900 or a year or two later.

---

١ — يعص الله تعالي ذذا لمن بني بيتاً في سبيل الله

٢ — (بنا.) والمبارك بتاريخ السابع و العشرين من شهر رمضان

٣ — × و تسعمائه من الهجرة النبوية في (زمان) السلطان العادل (ومكرم)

٤ — × المفخر ركن الدنيا والدين معزالاسلام و المسلمين ظل الله (في الارض)

٥ — والمظفر علي الاعداء الملك المويد ابي النصرة محمود بن احمد خلد الله

٦ — ملكه و اعلي امره و صار في مدينة سومنات جعليا لانه من بلاد الاسلام (وهدم)

٧ — الكفر والاصنام و امار حاكمها كتدبير بدر و مشيره بالراي الصائب المحفوظ

٨ — و ساعي الجهد والتخير و وهبه ايضا احقر العبد حاكم المذكور المسمي جانباز دمير

٩ — بن راوت (ثانمية) مع كبرلهم (ا) اول (فيهم ذيلك) فهو والثاني بمسره فاكثرو و الثالث

١٠ — (فتزودو) و الرابع زاهد و كلهم انفقوا جميعا علي تاسيس ذذ المسجد المعظم الاعلي

١١ — اسعد الدرجات بالصفة الصفا في السمعة السعيد عمدة المتقى و الدين اجمعوا الاسلام

١٢ — والمسلمين ابي الملوك و السلاطين السلاطين الاكابر الاعظم بردان المعتصم ملك جودر ملك الملوك و العبد

١٣ — والوفا خاقان الجود و السخا ابي ابراهيم بن محمد × نورالله مرقدد و طيب مسكنه مضجعه

14 ـــلامر ربي صاحب هذه المسجد وهو مصدرالمكرم الكريم سلطان المواخذ ملك ملوك

15 ـــ(حامي) التجار معزالدنيا والدين شمس الاسلام والمسلمين ابي الملوك والسلاطين ملجأ الاكابر

16 ـــوالامائل انتخارالعصر فيروز بن مبارك زادالله تعالي ادام الله في العز وثقاء و وقف

17 ـــعلي هذاالمسجد المذكورة المشهور (في جميع الكونين) (وهو) يبشر مع عاقبة جميعالوجه

18 ـــالله الكريم (قديما وانه لحليم) × × ذالك لصبنيا لعمارة هذا المسجد

19 ـــالمعظم ليكون العمارة لايمانا للاديان وانما بالامر الفرقان حبيب قال انما يعمر مساجد

20 ـــالله من آمن بالله واليوم الاخر واقام الصلواة وآتي الزكواة ولمن خشي الله نعسي

21 ـــاولئك ان يكونوا من المهتدين وانادة الانام و مودية و الفاضل عما عهدية

22 ـــيميل الي مكه حرسها الله و مدينة رسول الله علي الله عليه حتي يصرف في

23 ـــالسبيل من جميع التصرف فمن تصرف يقال طالبالتخير او يسعي في افساده يقول او نشاء

24 ـــاو ايماء او اشارة يعلم الله تعالي ذالك من التصميم لو ان مصمم اعتقاده

25 ـــ(لعنة) الله ولعنة الداعين و الملائكة والناس اجمعين فمن بده يعلمه

26 ـــالله علي الدين يبدلونه ان الله سميع عليم وحوالة

27 ـــعلي الله تعالي كماقال في محكم كتابه الكريم ان الله

28 ـــوصلي الله علي سيدنا محمد و آله الطيبين

God will pardon him who built a house in the way of God! This blessed building was constructed on the 27th of Ramjan A.H. (9* *). In the time of Mahomud, son of Ahmed, may God perpetuate his kingdom and exalt his rule! the just, the generous, and great king; the pillar of the religion and the State; the (honour of Islam and the Mussalmans; may God protect his territory! the king victorious over enemies and aided (by God); the father of victory.

He went to the town of Somnâth, which he turned into an Islamite city, and broke the power of the idols as well as infidelity. He appointed a governor, whose management was as able as that of the full moon; and made one counsellor, sensible, straightforward, fortunate, and industriously endeavouring after good:

8

also Hamir, son of Rawat, mean slave of the abovementioned governor, ready to sacrifice his life as his ancestors   *   *   *   *   *   *   *

 Firstly,   *   *   *   *   Secondly,   *   *   *   *   * Thirdly, increase!   Fourthly, practise abstinence and charity; and spend all in building this great high mosque! Malek Javer, of good rank, virtuous, auspicious, the pillar of truth and religion, the sum total of Islam and Mussalmans, the father of kings, the king of kings, the great nobleman, the strong reasoner, king of the kings of promise and fidelity, king of liberality and generosity, (viz.:) Abu Ibrahim, son of Mahomed, may God illumine his tomb! May He make his abode pleasant!

 By the order of my master, Firoz, son of Mubarek, may God increase and perpetuate his glory and his faith! The very fountain of generosity and liberality; the king avoiding punishments, the king of kings; the protector of merchants; the honour of religion and the world; the sun of Islam and the Moslems; the father of kings and sultans; the refuge of the great and the chosen; the ornament of the age!

 A pious bequest was made for this mosque in order to gain renown in both the worlds. And he gives the good news of the good end to all! For the sake of the generous God, Who is ancient and really meek!

 The construction of this great mosque will prove to be the edifice of faith and religion, by all means.—And surely there is no injunction of the Koran.

 God said (in the Koran) "He only shall build mosques for God who believe in God and the last day; and is constant at prayer, and pays the legal alms, and fears God above." These perhaps may become of the number of those who are rightly directed   *   *   *   *   *.

 May God preserve Mecca! he who is longing for Mecca and Medina of the prophet, so much so that he spends most in that way; and he who spent thus is a well-wisher.-   *   *   *   *   *.

 And God knows the person who tries to frustrate His design, either by word or sign or insinuation, however strong his faith may be. He shall be accursed by God, by angels, by men, and by all those who execrate such a deed.

 But he who shall change the legacy after he had heard it bequeathed by the dying person, surely the sin thereof shall be on those who change it, for God is He Who hears and knows.

 Confidence in the high God, as has been said in the Koran!

 May the blessing of God be on Mahomed, our chief and his holy progeny.

31

STONE INSCRIPTION IN THE DÂDÂ HARI'S VÂV AT AHAMADÂBÂD.

Dated A.H. 906.

This Vâv is in Haripurâ, a suburb of Ahamadâbâd, the capital town of the Mahomedan kings of Gujarât. In one of its side-walls is built up a piece of white-marble, into which this inscription is cut. It measures 22 ″×14″ and contains nine lines of Arabic, of which some letters at the end have become quite indistinct. It is there said that the magnificent building was constructed in the reign of Sultan Mahmûd Bigarha of Gujrât in the year A.H. 906, A.D. 1500.

١—شد هذه العمارة الظريفة و البقعة الشريفة

٢—والرواق الرفيعة و الصدر الا بعدن المصوره و عرش

٣—الاشجار الثمرة بالفواكهة مع البير و البركة

٤—ولشفيع الناس ملكا بنا في عهد سلطان سلاطين

٥—الزمان الواثق بتائيد الرحمان مزيد حيا و الايمان ابو الفتح

٦—محمود شاه بن محمد شاه ابن احمد شاه ابن محمد شاه بن مظفر شاه

٧—السلطان خلدالله ملكه (وامره) سلطان (وفي)

٨—جعلبا النصرة (النصيبا)   x . x

٩—المحروسة في الثاني ماه جمادي الاول سنه سته وتسعمايه

Finished: This graceful building and the noble place and the high portico and the flowing (water) like the Garden of Eden, and the alcove of fruitful and fruit-bearing trees together with the well and reservoir, (which) of course will make the people like them, (were) constructed in the time of the Sultan of the Sultans of the age, the firm, the God-aided, the increase of modesty, the faithful, the father of victory—Mahmûd Shah, son of Mahamad Shah, son of Ahmed Shah, son of Mahamad Shah, son of Muzzefir Shah, the Sultan (may God perpetuate his kingdom and his rule!)   *   *

May victory be his portion !   *   *   *

Preserved in writing : the 2nd of the month of Jemad-ul-awwal 906 A.H.

STONE INSCRIPTION IN MUJAFFER'S MASJID AT PAṬANA.

Dated A.H. 910.

This *masjid* is near the graveyard outside the western gate of Pâtana under
Junâgadh, and in it there is a piece of white stone bearing this inscription. Its
outer surface measures 21″ × 13″ containing six lines of mixed Persian and
Arabic composition, though some of the letters are not clear enough. It is said in
the inscription the mosque was caused to be built by one Sayed Jafar in the reign
of Sultan Mahmûd Bigarha of Gujarât in the year A.H. 910, A.D. 1504.

١ ـ بسم الله الرحمن الرحيم قال الله تعالي و ان المساجد لله

٢ ـ فلا تدعوا مع الله احدا وقال النبي صلي الله

٣ ـ عليه وسلم من بني مسجدًا بني الله له قصرًا في الجنة بناكرد

٤ ـ اين مسجد حقير بندئي شاه محمود سيد جعفر بنا كرد بمقرب

٥ ـ پروردگار (ميان حكيم سيد بن صاحب) سنه عشر تسعمايه شهر ربيع الاول گنشت

٦ ـ (تهانه دار قصبه كمباية)

In the name of God, the merciful and compassionate. God, the Most High, said :
" Verily the places of worship are set apart unto God : wherefore invoke not any
other therein together with God. "

The prophet (may the blessing and peace of God be on him !) said : " God will
build a palace for him in paradise who built a mosque for God. "

This mosque is made by *Sayed Jaffer*, a mean slave of King Mahmúd, for
Mia Hakim Sayed bin Sahib, waiting upon God. Made in the month of Rabi-ul-
awwal of the year 910 A.H.

Thanadar of the town of Cambay (*Kambayet*).

STONE INSCRIPTION AT THE GATE CALLED THE GRAND GATE AT PÂṬAṈA.

Dated A.H. 950.

This stone is built up in the town wall to the left of the gate and inside the town. It is a yellowish hard stone with its outer surface measuring 24" × 9". It contains eighteen lines of Persian with some of the letters broken and indistinct. it is a proclamation from Sultan Ahamad Shah forbidding the officials as well as non-officials from taking beddings, &c., from the ryots while on tour with a curse on both the Mussalmans and Hindus who may disobey this order. It is dated A.H. 950, A.D. 1543.

1 ‒ × × × × ×

2 ‒ بعهد سلطان الاعظم المعظم الوائق

3 ‒ تائيد الرحمن قطب الدنيا و الدين ابو

4 ‒ المظفر احمد شاه بن محمد شاه بن احمد شاه

5 ‒ بن محمد شاه بن مظفر شاه سلطان

6 ‒ عهددداران كوتوالي (و عبده داران مكيبا نرا) بدانند

7 ‒ كه بآمدن اينراه ازخانه كسي خلقىالله (كبلي)

8 ‒ مي كشيدند بر ايشان حرج و ظلم و تعد ي

9 ‒ و فعلي نا مشروع ميشد باثناي كارشاه

10 ‒ (و تاجر و عملداران ومنزلگيران و عبده

11 ‒ داران برگشته) سوداگران و مهاجنان

12 ‒ × × بي مشروع دور كنند اگر

13 ‒ (ثانياً حال از عهددداران) ازمسلم و كافر (كسيكه) (باشد)

14 ‒ (بي اذن ندهند) براي مسلمانرا (هركه برعهده آيد)

15 ‒ (سوكند) خداي شكسته باشد وبراي كافر را بوكند

16 ‒ سربتي و بت شود كه مي پرستند شكسته باشد تا خلقىالله

17 ‒ (آزار) × × × × × × × ×

18 ‒ × × × × × × شهر ذيالقعد سنه خمسين و تسعمايه

ماه محرم تاريخ اول سنه ۴۷۹

9

In the reign of Ahmedshah, the greatest and honoured Sultan, the firm, the God-aided, the pole-star of the world and the faith, the father of victory, son of Mahomed Shah, son of Ahmedshah, son of Mahomedshah, son of Sultan Muzzeffer Shah. Be it known to the holders of the office of *kotewal* as well as *mukhi*, that while travelling this way (they) used to carry away (*khaṭali*) from the houses of people, which led to crime, oppression, violence, and acts forbidden by religion in the course of imperial work ; and that traders, officials, persons encamping, the retired officers, merchants, and the Mahajan should abstain from doing such forbidden (deeds) ; and that if henceforth any of the officers, whether Mussalman or infidel, send for (such things) without permission, the Mussalman officer shall have abjured the oath of God and the infidel shall have abjured the oath of *Sarasvati* or the idol they may happen to worship, so that the creatures of God   *   *   *   *

The month of Zilcad, 950 A.H.

STONE INSCRIPTION OF THE MASJID AT LOLIÂNÂ.

Dated A.H. 968.

Loliânâ, where this mosque is, is a small village under Walla (the ancient Valabhipur) about twelve miles west of it. The mosque appears to have been built long before the date of the inscription, but it having fallen down, Sultan Mahmud Shah III. of Gujarât ordered it to be rebuilt. This inscription refers to the rebuilding of the mosque in A.H. 968, A.D. 1560-61. The stone is a white marble slab with an outer surface of 23″ × 13″, and contains five lines of mixed Arabic and Persian.

1 — بسم الله الرحمن الرحيم

2 — قال الله تعالي فان المساجد لله فلا تدعوا مع الله احدا ۵ ازين قبل

3 — عمدة الملک السلطان في دام الملک بنا کرده بود بعد (رجي با الله) (صاحب) (گردانيده بود) بعد (خادم شاه)

4 — هنجار و بيخار (بحکم) در عهد سلطان المحمد شاه (اين عمارت شکسته شده بود باز تيار کرده) اجر الله تعالي

5 — في الدارين باد ۵ (اميد از قاضي الحاجات است) (في) سنه ثمانيه و ستين سبعمايه

In the name of God, the merciful and compassionate.

God, the Most High, said : Verily the places of worship are set apart unto God ; wherefore invoke not any other therein together with God.

Before this time it was made by Um-dat-ul-mulk (the pillar of the State) of the Sultan of the enduring kingdom ; afterwards (Rajiyellah) Saheb made alterations ; then, in the reign of Sultan Mahmad Shah, this building having fallen down, a servant of the king (full of manners and without fear), repaired it by order : May God reward him in both the worlds ! Be it so ! Hope is from the Judge of the necessities (God). In the year * 968 A.H.

STONE INSCRIPTION OF THE SHRINE OF HASSAN PIR OF TALÂJÂ.

Dated A.H. 974.

This shrine is in the form of an *eda-gah* to the west of the small town of Talâjâ, known in ancient history as Taladhvaja, under Bhavnagar, about thirty-five miles south of it. In the wall of the *eda-gah* there is a hard black stone bearing this inscription in eight lines, the letters of which have become rather indistinct. It mentions the building of a mosque by Sayed Sadik in the time of Sultan Muzeffer Shah, who, it says, was the last of the rulers of the country (Gujarât). It bears the date A.H. 974, A.D. 1566-67.

١ ـــ بسم الله الرحمن الرحيم

٢ ـــ وان المساجد لله فلا تدعوا مع الله احدا ه

٣ ـــ اشهد ان لا (اله) الا الله وحده لاشريك له و اشهد

٤ ـــ ان محمدا عبده و رسوله اين مسجد تيار كرده براٸي سيد صادق

٥ ـــ بن سيد كمال الدين بن سيد جميل الدين بن سيد عاظم بن سيد ميران

٦ ـــ بن سيد محمود بن يداالله بن مخدوم جها نيان صاحب عالم بتغاري

٧ ـــ در آخر مجموع حاكم حين سلطان مظفر شاه بن سلطان محمود شاه

٨ ـــ سلطان احمد شاه سلطان محمود شاه محمد شاه بهادر شاه محمود شاه بن
سلطان مظفر شاه غفراالله

---

* The year 768 A.H. seems to be incorrect, because there was no Mahomedan king of Gujrat at all then.

Dated the first of the month of Mohurrum, 974 A.H.

In the name of God, the merciful and compassionate. " Verily the places of worship are set apart unto God ; wherefore invoke not any other therein together with God.

" I bear witness to this that there is no God but God, who is one and without any partner, and I bear witness to this that Mahomed is really his slave and messenger." This mosque was built by Seyd Sadik, son of Seyd Kamal-ud-din, son of Seyd Jamil-ud-din, son of Seyd Azim, son of Seyd Miran, son of Seyd Mahmud, son of Yad-dullah, son of Makhdum Jehanian Saheb Alum of Bokhara ; in the reign of the last of all the rulers of the time, (that is) Sultan Muzeffer Shah, son of Sultan Mahmud Shah, (son of) Sultan Ahmed Shah, son of Mahmud Shah, (son of) Mahomed Shah, (son of) Bahadurshah, (son of) Mahamud Shah son of Sultan Muzeffer Shah. May God pardon him !

STONE INSCRIPTION OF THE NEW MASJID OF THE KAJIS AT PÂTANA.

Dated A.H. 976.

This is one of the two inscriptions in the Kaji's new *masjid* at Pâtana, better known as Somanâth Pâtana, on the south-west coast of Kâthiâwâd. The stone is a piece of white marble with an outer surface measuring 24" × 6". It contains three lines and the letters are well preserved. The inscription is written in Persian mixed with Arabic. It is said that the mosque was built in the reign of Sultan Mahamud Shah* in A.H. 976, A.D. 1568-69.

---

١ — بسم الله الرحمن الرحيم قال الله تعالي و ان المساجد لله فلا تدعوا مع الله
احدا ه

٢ — وقال النبي علي الله عليه وسلم من بني مسجداً بني الله له قصراً في الجنة

٣ — بنامنهاد اين مسجد بنده گناهگار حضرت پرورد گار الراجي الي الله محمود
بن عنمان بن. حاجي بن اعتماد الملك شهر شوال سنه ٦٧٩ سبعين تسعمايه

* Muzeffer Shah III.

In the name of God, the merciful and compassionate. God the Most High said : " Verily the places of worship are set apart unto God ; wherefore invoke not any other therein together with God. " And the prophet (may the blessing and peace of God be on him !) said : " God will build a palace for him in paradise who builds a mosque for Him (here)." This mosque is built by Mahmud bin Osman bin Haji bin It-mad-ul-mulk, the sinful slave of the exalted God, in whom lies his hope of all. The month of Shawwal A.H. 976.

STONE INSCRIPTION IN THE PÂNCH BIBI'S BASTION (KOTHÂ) AT PÂTAṆA.

Dated A.H. 977.

This stone, which is a white marble slab, being built up in the wall and being inside the bastion, is in a good state of preservation. It measures 24″ × 8″ and contains five lines of Persian mixed with Arabic. From the contents it seems that the inscription refers to the building of a mosque in the time of Sultan Mahmud * Shah of Gujarât in the year A.H. 977, A.D. 1569-70.

١—بسم الله الرحمن الرحيم قال الله تعالي وان المساجد لله فلا تدعوا مع الله احدا ٥
وقال النبي صلي الله عليه وسلم من بني مسجدًا بني الله له نصرًا في الجنة
بنا كرد

٢—اين مسجد بنده گناهگار حضرت پروردگار الراجي الي الله بده بن كل بن
كمال بن اده بن فتح (لا يندده) گجرات اسلاته دار سلطان الاعظم المعظم الوائق

٣—بالله المنان ناصرالدنيا والدين ابوالفتح محمود شاه بن محمد شاه بن احمد
شاه بن محمد شاه بن مظفرشاه السلطان خلد الله ملكه

٤—وثبت دولته هركه بيايد وبر بيند دعا ايمان اين حقيرا ياد باشند تا نواب
وثمرات در نامة اونبت افتد آمين رب العالمين تمة

٥—شد اين بخطه العبد النقيص النحيف الراجي الي رحمة الله الكريم جمال بن
اسماعيل بن احمد غفرالله له وآله اجمعين يوم الربعا التاسع عشر من رجب
سنه سبع وسبعين وتسعمايه   × ×

In the name of God, the merciful and compassionate.

God the High said : " Verily the places of worship are set apart for God ; wherefore invoke not any other therein together with God."

---

* Muzeffer Shah III.

The prophet (may the blessing and peace of God be on him!) said : " God will build a palace for him in paradise who builds a mosque for God (here). " This mosque was built by Budeh bin Gul bin Kamal bin Ladha bin Fateh (of) Gujarât, the sinful slave of the exalted God, one who hopes from God, the arms-bearer to the great and magnificent Sultan, confiding in the beneficent God, the defender of the world and the faith, the father of victory, viz., Mahmud Shah bin Mahomed Shah bin Ahmed Shah bin Mahomed Shah bin Muzeffer Shah, the Sultan (may God perpetuate his kingdom ! may his fortune be constant !). May every one who comes here and sees this remember the name of this humble ser-vant with the blessing of faith ; so that its merit and profit be registered in his record ! (supposed to be kept by the angels). Oh, the Nourisher of the world, be it so ! Finished. This is done in the handwriting of Jemal bin Ismail bin Ahmed (may God pardon him and his progeny and all !), the feeble and insigni-ficant slave, hoping for mercy from God, the beneficent ! Dated Wednesday, the 29th of the month of Rajab * * A.H. 977.

STONE INSCRIPTION OF THE MAUSOLEUM OF AMIR BEG AT THARÂD.

Dated A.H. 1011.

This inscription is engraved round the tomb of Amir Beg, which is built of pure white marble. The mausoleum is at Tharâd, a town on the borders of the Raṇa, or sandy-desert, of Kutch, and to the north-east of it. It says that Amir Beg was a great martyr and died in A.H. 1011, (A.D. 1602,) when Emperor Akbar ruled at Delhi. It is written in a single line in Persian all round the tomb, and is 15 ft. 3 in. in length and 5 inches in breadth. The tomb, as well as the inscription, are in a good state of preservation.

1—الله محمد الله كافي زہي شيردل اميربيگ آنكہ تيغش تجويز بر اعدائي دين
جون بر آمد عدوي كہ جون كوہ بود است متحكم بيک لصاحب جون ہايم از
پا درآمد بروز وفا در صفوف دليران في التاريخ يازدہم ماہ رجب ۱۰۱۱ روز
دوشنبہ اميربيگ شہادت پيوست بہي تن ز دمغام او بي سر آمد باخر
بسر ماندہ تاج شہادت بنخلوتگہ آن جہاني در آمد پئي سال تاريخ اوعدد لبي
بگفتا ز باغ جہان گل بر آمد حسني نعمة ربي

God! Mahamed! God is sufficient! Bravo Amir Beg! When on the day of turmoil, his sword was raised from the ranks of the heroes in order to shed the blood of the enemies of the faith, the enemy, who was as firm as a rock, vanished like a shadow in a moment. On Monday, the 11th of the month of Rajab 1011 A. H., Amir Beg obtained martyrdom.

The heads of many persons were severed from the body by his sword ; at last the crown of martyrdom was left on his head. He entered the nook of retirement of the next world ; for the year of his date the nightingale said : " The flower emerged from the garden of the world." The value of these letters = 1011. Enough for me the happiness of my Nourisher !

STONE INSCRIPTION IN SADAR MIYÂN'S HOUSE AT MÂNGROL.
Dated A.H. 1033.

This inscription is engraved into a yellow marble slab in eight lines of Persian within an area of 16″ × 9″. This stone is built up in a wall of the upper storey of the house of Sadar Miyân at Mângrol on the south-west coast of Kâthiâwâḍ. It mentions the inhabiting of a suburb called Lâlapura, near the town, by one Lâla Beg, who appears to be an imperial officer at Mângrol at the time. It bears date the year A.H. 1033, (A.D. 1623-24,) when Emperor Jahangir was on the throne at Delhi.

الله

۱ — تا جهان را مدار بر گذر است

۲ — این بنا را قرار معتبر است

۳ — لعل بیگ امر در ان فرمود

۴ — لعل پور را کر معد نی گهر است

۵ — لعل غالب چو یافت تاریخش

۶ — دوتی زین حساب گنگ و کرست

۷ — روز شنبر بتاریخ بیست و سیم ماه رجب نوشته شد سنه ۱۰۳۳

God is most powerful ! As long as the world is revolving in its orbit this foundation is firmly fixed. Lal Beg thus ordered with regard to Lalpur, which is a mine of gems. When Lal (ruby) discovered its date to be " victorious " (Galib, 1033, a play upon words), the pearl became dumb and deaf by this calculation.

Saturday, the 23rd of the month of Rajab A. H. 1033,this was written.

Note.—*Lal* has here three meanings, viz., 1st, the name Lal Beg ; 2nd, the town Lalpur ; 3rd, a ruby.

STONE INSCRIPTION OF THE BÀVAN SABURI MASJID AT MÂNGROL.

Dated A.H. 1033.

The Bàvan Saburi's mosque, in which this inscription is found, is situated at Mângrol on the way to the *bunder* (harbour) from the town. The stone is a yellow marble piece containing nineteen lines in Persian within a space of 30″ × 12″. Several letters in the 13th, 17th, and 18th lines have been lost. It mentions the building of the mosque by one Amir Beg, who seems to be a military officer appointed in this province in the year A.H. 1033, (A.D. 1623-24,) during the reign of Emperor Jahangir.

الله اکبر رب یسر

1 ـــ ز زلف حور که جاروب داده این درگهر است

2 ـــ ازان ز نور صفا پر همیشه خواجه گهر است

3 ـــ نه روضه ایست مگر طارم مسیحا ایست

4 ـــ که یا چو برج شرف جلوه گاه مهر و مه است

5 ـــ بر آن شرف که ز نه کرسي فلک بخشید

6 ـــ بیک طواف درش حاصل گدا و شه است

7 ـــ جناب اوکه مقامات اهل دعا ایست

8 ـــ سحر و شام جهان با حق رهنمائي رهست

9 ـــ مدار عالم علویت بود امین مبارک را

10 ـــ مدد او بستارۀ سپاه و شهریاري هست

11 ـــ (بر غرب (و) صبح برینجا که ز حلق هست بدعاي)

12 ـــ (بدعاي) او همه کشور کشاینده امید است

13 ـــ نسیم × × × × بشگفد ازوي

14 ـــ مرا که غنچۀ (امید) ته بته است

15 ـــ جو بي باغل تاریخ روضه شد چکنم

سنه ۱۰۳۳

16 ـــ (برین صله صادر شد عقل بي ته است

17 ـــ (بسر شدي جو) × × × × × ×

18 ـــ که از × × × × ز برگ و × است

God is greatest! Oh, Nourisher, make it easy!

This court is swept with the ringlet of a hourie, hence it is that this place of the Lord is always filled with pure light.

It is no garden, but it is the abode of Jesus, or it is the place or the noble house whence the sun and the moon shine forth.

Owing to the nobility bestowed on it by the nine heavens, one circuit round the door fulfils the desire of the beggar as well as the king.

Its vestibule, where people assemble for prayers, is the guide of the world, morning and evening, to the path of God.

May Amin Mubarek be the centre of the exalted world. The fortune of the soldiers and the king is indebted to his help.

This place is for prayer on the part of the people, morning and evening.

His blessing is the opener of the world of hope.

The bud of my hope is full of folds, owing to the pleasant breeze which opens the flower of hope.

Since the date of this garden (२iळ) is unintentionally obtained from the words ("ba gul" 1033 A.H.) "with noise," what can I do?

This excellent reward is obtained. Wisdom is depthless.

STONE INSCRIPTION OF LÂLPURÂ AT MÂNGROL.
Dated A.H. 1033.

This inscription is cut into a hard, smooth, yellow stone, which is built up in the back wall of the house of one Sadar Miân, residing in Lâlpurâ, at Mângrol. It has a square face measuring 14″ × 14″, and contains six lines of Persian and five lines of Sanskrit. The latter portion is given in the Sanskrit portion of this work. It refers to the inhabiting of a new suburb called Lâlapurâ at Mângrol by one Lal Beg, who appears to be a dependent of Prince Akbar. The date given therein is A. H. 1033 (A. H. 1623-24), when the Emperor Jahângir was on the throne of Delhi.

شاهزاده حسن جهانگیر اکبر

لعل بیگ غلام (بادشاه) بتاریخ بستم شهر جمادی الاول سنه ۱۰۳۳ روز
دوشنبر از عنایت الهی لعل پوره آباد شد آنجم بهبودی و آبادان این پوره
باشد دران کوشش دریغ ندارند چیزے طمع نکنند اگر طمع میکرده باشد
خدا درمیانست هر حاکم که بیاید خبرداری میکرده باشند از برائی خدا

Prince Hasan Jehangir Akbar.

Lâlbeg, the slave of the king.

Lalpur became populated through the kindness of God, on Monday, the 20th of Jemadi-ul-awwal, A. H. 1033.

For the welfare and prosperity of this town, no pains are to be spared and no gains are to be coveted ; and if anybody becomes greedy, God is in view ; every governor coming here must keep himself informed for the sake of God.

STONE INSCRIPTION OF THE VÂV AT SELIMPURA, NEAR AHAMADABAD.

Dated A.H. 1035.

The *Vâv*, in which this inscription is found, is in Selimpura, near Ahamad-abad, on the way to it from Meywar. It is a white sandstone built up in the wall with a face measuring 22″ × 14″, and contains eleven lines of Persian. The stone, though inside the *Vâv*, has crumbled down a little by the effects of weather. It mentions that the work was begun by a Borah, named Suliman, in A.H. 1032 (A.D 1622-23), and was completed in A.H. 1035 (A.D. 1625-26), when Selim (Jehângir) was Emperor (of India) and Nawab Khan Jahan, son of Doulat Khan Lodi, was the Viceroy of Gujrât.

الله اكبر

١ ---- بحكم ايزد غفار و بعون حضرت كردكار سليمان ولد

٢ ---- داود ولد يوسف ابن محمد بودره ساكن قصبة

٣ ---- موراسه را توفيق رفيق شد تا حسبتاً لله وتمتعوا

٤ ---- لتخلق الله عمارة اين ما بين بتاريخ چهارم ماه

٥ ---- صفر روز خميس سنة ١٠٣٢ شروع نمود شد چون نيت صالح

٦ ---- بود بعنايت الله تعالي روز جمعه موافق بتاريخ ٢٩

٧ ---- بيست و نهم شهر شوال سنة ١٠٣٥ الف و خمس وثلاثين

٨ ---- درايام سلطنت سلطان سليم جهانگير بادشاه و

٩ ---- صاحب صوبگي نواب خانجهان ولد

١٠ ---- دولت خان لودهي و درجاگير داري خوبي

١١ ---- جهانيم خان دكني صورت اتمام يافت

God is most powerful.

At the command of God, the Forgiver, and with the help of the exalted Creator, divine grace became the guide of Suliman, son of Daud, son of Yusuf, son of Mahumad, a Borah, inhabitant of Kasbe Momasch, so that for the love of God and the benefit of God's creatures the construction of this was begun on the 4th day of the month of Saffar, Thursday, A.H. 1032. Since the intention was good it was completed, through the favour of God, the Most High, on Friday, corresponding to the 29th day of the month of Shavval, 1035 A.H., during the absolute dominion of Selim Jehangir, Emperor, and the viceroyalty of Nawab Khan Jahan, son of Doulat Khan Lodi, and the Jagirdari of Khubi Jehanim Khan Dekni.

STONE INSCRIPTION IN THE PALACE AT MÂNGROL.

Dated A.H. 1047.

This inscription stone is placed in the open terrace of the buildings called Badi Mâdi's residence at Mângrol. It is a common white sand-stone built up in the wall with the outer surface measuring 26″ × 13″. It contains four lines in Persian to the effect that the palace was built by Jamal Khan Nahani, a nobleman of the court of Emperor Shah Jehan, and who held Mângrol in jagir. It was built in A.H. 1047 (A.D. 1637.)

---

1 — بسم الله الرحمن الرحيم ا الر الا الله محمد الرسول الله

2 — در وقت خلافت بادشاه شاه جهان جمال خان نوحاني كر امراء باد

3 — شاهي بودند و پرگنه منگلور در جاگير داشتند دران ايام بتاريخ سنه هزار و

4 — چهل و هفت سراي بادشاهي بنا كردند در ماه رجب تاريخ دويم روز جمعه با تمام رسيد

"In the name of God, the merciful and compassionate. There is no god but God. Mahomed is the prophet of God." During the reign of the king Shah Jehan Jemal Khan Nuhani, who was a nobleman of the realm and had the puragneh (district) of Mângrol as his jagir, made this royal mansion in those times, dated 1047 ; it was finished on Friday, the 2nd of the month of Rajab.

STONE INSCRIPTION OF KILLA (FORT) SHÂHPUR AT RÂNPUR.

Dated A.H. 1048.

This inscription is cut into a piece of white marble measuring 10″ × 7″ with six lines in Persian, and is placed inside the fortress in the wall, so that the stone is well protected from the effects of weather. Fort Shâhpur, to the building of which the inscription refers, appears to have been erected for the protection of the town of Rânpur, an important place on the confines of Gujarât and Kâthiâvâḍ and a station on the Bhavnagar-Wadhwan Section of the B.-G. Railway. Though it does not contain the name of any ruler, yet from the name of the fort and the date, viz. 1048 (A.D. 1638), it appears that Emperor Shah Jehan was on the throne of Delhi.

نقل دروازۀ قلعه

خان کہ نوعروس جهان نمیجو او نزاد ١—خان معظم اعظم خان روزگار

خان بلند رتبہ کہ عمرش دراز باد ٢—شیر ژیان شجاع زمان سرور جهان

طبعی اگر ترا برسد در کم و زیاد ٣—گفتا بلطف خاص کہ تاریخ این حصار

امداد جستم از کرم خالق العباد ٤—تاریخ این بنا کہ ازو دور چشم بد

کردم رقم بجانم دل اعظم بلاد ٥—گشتم بہ بحر فکر شناور بنحکم او

| ١٠٤٨ | الله اکبر بمطابق شهر محرم الحرام سنہ هزار چهل و هشت هجری

The great honoured Lord (*Khan*), the Khan of the age. such as the new bride of the world has not given birth to.

The fierce lion, the warrior of the time, the chief of the world. the Khan of great dignity ; may he live long !

The Khan, with special kindness, asked me to compose the date of this fortress long or short, as I liked.

For the date of this building—may the evil eye be far from it ! I sought the help of the Creator of slaves

At his command I began to swim in the sea of thought : I wrote with my soul and heart " the greatest city " (that is, 1048).

God is greatest. In the honoured month of Mohurrum, A.H. 1048.

INSCRIPTION No. 2 IN THE SAME FORT.

Dated A.H. 1050.

This inscription is also in the same fort, of equal size and equally well preserved, but it contains three lines and a half in Persian to the effect that Azim Khan, Viceroy of Gujarât, caused a mosque to be built in that fort in the year A.H. 1050 (A.D. 1640).

نقل مسجد قلعه

1—در عهد بادشاه جمجاه عادل باذل شهاب الدين محمد صاحبقران ثاني شاه
جهان بادشاه غازي

2—خلد الله ملكه و ابدا در شهر ذي الحجه سنه هزار پنجاه هجري نيازمند
درگاه كبريائے الهي اعظم خان در زمان صاحب

3—صوبگي گجرات اين مسجد متبرک را در اين قلعه شاهپور بنا نهاد و باختتام
رسانيد كه عباد الله عبادت معبود بر حق مينموده باشند

In the time of Shahabuddin Mahomed, the king of the dignity of Jamshed, just, generous, the second Tamerlane, the king of the world, the king who warred for Islam; may God perpetuate his kingdom for ever!

In the month of Zil-Haj, 1050 A.H., the petitioner, at the court of the great God, viz., Azim Khan, laid the foundation of this blessed mosque within the fort of Shahpur when he was Viceroy (*subah*) of Gujarât and completed it in order that the slaves of God may continue to worship the true God.

INSCRIPTION No. 3 IN THE SAME FORT.

Dated A.H. 1051.

This is also a companion inscription, equally well preserved in the same fort. It contains only two lines in Persian mentioning the sinking and building of a well by the abovementioned Viceroy of Gujarât in the year A.H. 1051 (A.D. 1641).

12

نقل چاه بر لب جو نیست

1 ــ در شهر شوال سنه هزار پنجاه یک هجری نیازمند درگاه کبریائی الهی اعظم
خان در زمان صاحب صوبگی گجرات

2 ــ این چاه را بنا ساخت وقف این باغ نمود که خلق الله زمان مشرف شوند
والسلام

In the month of Shawal, A.H. 1051, Azim Khan, a petitioner at the court of the great God, having made this well when he was Viceroy of Gujarât (*subah*), gave it in charity in connection with this garden, so that the creatures of God may take advantage of it. Peace!

INSCRIPTION No. 4 IN THE SAME FORT.
Dated A.H. 1052.

This is the fourth inscription placed in the same fort, to commemorate the building of a *Hamam* (bath) by the same Viceroy during his tenure of office in A.H. 1052 (A.D. 1642).

نقل حمام قلعه

الله اکبر

1 ــ نیازمند درگاه الهی اعظم خان در زمان صاحب صوبگی گجرات این حمام
درین عمارت را بتاریخ غره

2 ــ در شهر جمادی الآخر سنه ۱۰۵۱ هزار پنجاه یک شروع نمود در شهر محرم
الحرام سنه هزار پنجاه و دو

3 ــ بر اختتام رسانید هر که باین مقام برسند بذکر خیر یاد کنند

Azim Khan, the petitioner at the court of the great God, made this bath (*Hamamkhanah*) when he was Viceroy of Gujarât.

It was begun on the 1st of Jamad-ul-Akbar, 1051 A.H., and completed in the honoured month of Mohurrum, A.H. 1052. Whoever comes here may bless (me)!

STONE INSCRIPTION IN THE DARBÂR GADH OR CHIEF'S PALACE AT MÂNGROL.

Dated A.H. 1097.

The part of the palace where this inscription is placed is called *Ghâvd Khâná,* a place where the sepoys on guard take their tea, coffee, &c. It is beside a mosque called the Râvali *musjid* at Mângrol, on the west coast of Kâthiâvâḍ. The stone is a piece of white marble, 16″ × 15″, with ten lines in Persian, of which some letters have become indistinct. A notice was issued in the time of the Emperor Aurangzeb by Shahverdikhan, Governor of Sorath, that the merchants should not be compelled to purchase the produce of the jagirdars in whole lots. It is dated A.H. 1097 (A.D. 1685-86).

پادشاه هو الفياض

چون بندهٔ درگاهِ خلایق پناه شاهوردیخان بحفظ و حراست این سر زمین
رسیده مطلع شد که حکام پیشین غلات جاگیر خود را بطرح یعنی اود هره بر بیوپاریان
داده روا دار نقصان آنها می شدند و ابواب ممنوعه از قسم فروخیات بجبراً می
گرفتند بتوفیق ایزدی این خیرخواه خلق الله بتصدی عمر دین پناه قرار داده که
غلر را بطریق اود هره بر بیوپاریان ندهم و ابواب ممنوعه نگیرم چون این امریست
دال بر سرخروئی دنیا و عقبیٰ لهذا آسانی میکنم که حکام آینده منصوب آبا نیز غلر
را بعلت اود هره بر بیوپاریان ندهند و غیره ابواب ممنوعه از رعایا
وغیره نگیرند وهرکس که × جز این باب راضی خواهد شد او را قسم قرآن
مجید ست وبرا وطلای خواهد افتاد وبالتوفیق شیئی عزیز او یفعل الله × × ×
× × پانزدهم شهر ربیع الاول سنه هزار نود و هفت

The Liberal King.

When Shahverdikhan, the slave of the court of the protector of the people, became the guardian and custodian of this region, he came to know that his predecessors in office used to sell all sorts of grain of their jagir by force, that is, by giving it to the merchants for a lump sum (*udhad*); they approved of the loss the latter were put to; and also levied prohibited imposts and so on. By the grace of God, this well-wisher of the people of God, determined by way of sacrifice for the life of the protector of religion, " I would not sell grain by wholesale nor would I receive forbidden imposts." " Since this deed leads to honour in this world as well as the next, I make it easy (by laying it down) that the future governors, appointed by the elders also, should not give any grain to the merchants by the wholesale system, nor receive any forbidden imposts from the ryots and others ; any one who will take pleasure in doing otherwise shall have abjured the glorified Koran and will be repudiated (by God)."

Success is from God : it is a dear thing ＊ ＊ ＊

The 15th day of the month of Rajab-ul-Awwal, A.H. 1097.

STONE INSCRIPTION IN THE MARKET SQUARE AT PRABHÂS PÂṬAN.
Dated A.H. 1097.

This inscription is also to the same effect as the one above, and was caused to be placed by the same officer in the wall of a shop in the market square at Prabhâs Pâṭâna, better known as Somanâth Pâṭâna, on the south-west coast of Kâthiâvâḍ. The date is also the same, viz., A.H. 1097 (A.D. 1685-86).

يا فتاح

چون بندۀ درگاه خلايق بناۀ شاهزرديخان بحفظ وحراست اين سر زمين رسيده مطلع شد كه حكام پيشين غلات جاگير خود را بطرح بيني يعني بر بيوپاريان داده روادار نقصان آنها ميشدند و ابواب ممنوعه از قسم فروخيات وغيره مي گرفتند بر اين امر چون اين خيرخواه خلق باشد بر تصدق بادشاه در بيبار قرارداد كه مكرراً منكرين امربيوپاريان جميع ابواب ممنوعه نگيرم چون اين امريست مكرم بسرخروي دنيا و عقبي لهذا مهنائي ميكنم كه آئنده از حكام منصوب اينجا غلهرا اودهره بر بيوپاريان ندهند و فروخيات وغيره ابواب ممنوعه از رعايا نگيرند و هركس آئنده جزاين ابواب راضي خواهد شد اورا قسم قرآن مجيد است و براوطلاق انتاد في ايل دوازدهم شهر ربيع الاول سنه ۱۰۹۷

O ! the Opener !

When Shahverdikhan, the slave of the court of the protector of the people became the guardian and custodian of this territory, he was informed that the preceding governors used to sell all sorts of grain of their jagheer to the merchants forcibly for a lump sum and thus approved of their losses ; also used to receive forbidden taxes by way of (*farukhyat*), and so on.   Upon this (I), the well-wisher of the people of God, resolved, by way of a sacrifice for the king, the defender of the faith, that this humble servant should not collect any of the forbidden imposts from the merchants, and since this is an act honoured for the respect (it obtains) in this world as well as the next, I prohibit the appointed governors of this place, in future also, from selling any grain to the merchants by force for a lump sum (*udhad*) ; and (also) from receiving any (*farukhyat*) and other forbidden imposts from the ryots. And if anybody, in future, will take delight in doing otherwise, he shall have abjured the Koran and be repudiated (by God).   Written in the year 1097 A.H. on the 12th of the month of Rabi-ul-awwal.

STONE INSCRIPTION IN THE SHRINE OF HAZRAT PIR AT GHOGHÂ.

Dated A.H. 1146.

The shrine of Hazrat Pir in which this inscription is found is situated on the seaside at Ghoghâ, a British port on the eastern coast of Kâthiâvâḍ.   It is cut into a white soft stone and has eight lines of Persian mixed with Arabic.   The surface of the stone measures 10″ × 8″.   It refers to the building of a mosque by a Ṭaṇḍel (the head officer in a ship) named Bapuji in the year A.H. 1146, A.D. 1733, during the reign of Emperor Mahomed Shah of Delhi.

1—بسم الله الرحمن الرحيم لا اله الا الله محمد الر

2—سول الله فلاتدعوا مع الله احدا ميمنت مانو

3—س بادشاه جهان خليفة الرحمان محمد شاه

4—جهان گير خلد الله ملكه و سلطانه مطابق

5—سنه احدي من هجرت محمد مصطفيٰ علي الله عليه

6—و سلم شير ربيع الاول سنه ١١٤٦ مسجد آراسته

7—بايوجي بن موسي جي تنڊيل خليفه قادري (بدر)

8—شاه ولد (كاظم علي) ميان شاه سعيد بن ×

In the name of God the merciful and compassionate :

There is no god but God ; Mahomed is the prophet of God :

Therefore invoke not any other therein together with God.

Mahomed Shah, the conqueror of the world, the favourite of fortune, the king of the world, the Khalif of God ; may God perpetuate his kingdom and rule !

This mosque was made by Tandel Bapuji, son of Musaji, a Khalif (deputy) of Kaderi Badrshah, son of Kazim Ali Mian Shah Syed, son of   * * * in the year corresponding to that of the flight of Mahomed, the chosen ; may the blessing and peace of God be on him ! viz., in the month of Rabi-ul-awwal, A.H. 1146.

STONE INSCRIPTION AT THE GÂDI GATE AT MÂNGROL.

Dated A.H. 1162.

This inscription stone is a white marble slab measuring 27″ × 12″. It is built up in the wall to the left side of the gate at Mângrol on the west coast of Kâthiâvâḍ. The inscription is written in Persian and mentions the capturing of the fort of Mângrol, which had fallen into the hands of the Marathas, by Sheikh Fakhruddin and Malik Shahbuddin in A.H. 1162, A.D.1 749, when the central power at Delhi had collapsed and the Marathas had become powerful in the land.

1—بسم الله الرّحمن الرحيم

2—بعد از حمد ايزد بر حق ودرود نا محدود

3—رسول مطلق مشهود اهل شهود باد كر بعد

4—فتح مخدوم سيد سكندر در قلعه قصبه منگلور

5—مدت ممتد مشعل اسلام روشن بود رفته

6—رفته در تصرف كفاركهين رفته و تا مدت

7—دوازده سال اطوار ظلم چنان جارى بودند

8—كه اكثر جمهور يكنه رو بفرار نهادند الحمد لله كه

9—بتائيد آسمانى در سنه يازده صد و شصت و دو

51

10 — سال من هجرة النبوي همین حصن اكابران
11 — قصبه منگلور باسم ملک شهاب الدین و شیخ
12 — فخر الدین و بعد اخوان ایشان بتاریخ بیست و
13 — سیوم شهر رمضان المبارک روز یکشنبه بوقت ظهر
14 — فتح کرده بنای اسلام بریا نمودند سنه ۱۱۶۲
کتبه حافظ موسی تهتی

In the name of God, the merciful and compassionate.

After praising God, the truthful, and blessing the absolute prophet, be it known to the righteous people, that for a long time after the conquest of the fortress of the town of Mânglore (Mângrol) by H. E. Sayed Sikandar, the torch of Islam having burnt bright, it (the fortress) gradually passed away into the hands of the unbelievers of the Dekkhan ; and that for a period of twelve years such modes of oppression had prevailed as made numbers of the inhabitants flee away.

God be praised, that by divine help, this very fortress having been conquered by the great ones of the town of Mânglore (Mângrol) such as Malik Shahbuddin Shekh Fakhruddin, and some of their brethren, at the time of noon, on Sunday, the 23rd of the blessed month of Ramjan, A.H. 1162, the foundation of Islam was laid.

This was written by Hafiz Musa Thathi.

STONE INSCRIPTION OF THE MEHMUDÂBÂD GATE AT RÂDHANAPUR.
Dated A.H. 1191.

This inscription-stone is built up in the wall near the Mehmudâbâd Gate at Râdhanapur, a small independent Mahomedan principality in the Pâlanpur agency and north-west of Ahmadâbâd. The stone measures 22″ × 15″ and contains seven lines, of which five lines are written in the usual way, one line on its left side and one below. The inscription is written in Persian and mentions the inhabiting of a new town called Pâdshahpur by Khân Najmuddin Gazi in A.H. 1191, A.D. 1777.

هو الصمد

چو دولت رام کرده مهمازی	1—بحکم خان نجم الدین غازی
تمامی خلق از دل گشت راضی	2—شده آباد شهری پادشاه پور
کہ بانی را شود عمر درازی	3—بر درگر ایزدی شکرانه کردند
رعایا میکند چون طفل بازی	4—بزیر سایہ لطفش تا بصد سال
بر دینا ناتھہ شد بندہ نوازی	5—بسال الف وصد تسعین و واحد

1—پنجم شهر صفر المظفر سنہ ۱۱۹۲ هجری راقم و مصنف دینا ناتھہ منشی باهتمام محمد پناہ داروغہ بکارسازی گلکار بهگوان و روبا

2—دروازہ طرف مشرقی مرتب عاقبت بخیر باد

(He is Eternal.)

The city of Padshahpoor became populated by order of Khan Najmud-din Gazi, when Fortune, which does great works, became obedient to him ; all the people were glad from their hearts, and thankfully prayed to God that the founder may live long and that the ryots may play like children for a century together under the shadow of his kindness.

This kindness was shown to Dinnanath in the year 1191 (A.H.). The 5th of the month of Saffer, the Victorious, A.H. 1192. Dinnanath Munshi, the composer and writer, with the effort of Mahamed Panah, the darogeh and Bhagwan and Rupa, employed in the earth-work, this eastern gate was erected. May the result be good !

STONE INSCRIPTION OF THE BHILOT GATE AT RÁDHANPUR.
Dated A.H. 1192.

This inscription relates to the inhabiting of the same town by the same officer. It is inscribed on a white marble slab with a surface of 41″ × 12″ containing five lines, and which is placed near the Bhilot Gate at Rádhanpur. It is dated A.H. 1192, A.D. 1778.

١٥٣

هوالصمد

١ — ز جوی صفائی عمارت خلعتِ هندستان است
بر بادشاه پور دایم خدا نگهبان است
بحکم خان نجم الدین و بادشاه بیگم
کز فیضی بتخش رعایا و غریبان است
همهٔ خلائق در عشرتِ فراوان است

٢ — نجور و ظلم بر احوال هیچکس کاهی
بذوق کسب بیوپار خود نمایان است
حصار گشت بنا باکمال استحکام
کز از صلابت آن دشمنان گریزان است
ز صدقِ باطن دپراپ رام متصدی
تردداتِ کنان همچو اهل ایقان است

٣ — بحال کارکنان و غریب مزدوران
بوقتِ شام گهربار همچون نیسان است
هزار سال بفرخندگی مبارکباد
تمام خلقی بدین ورد حرف گویان است
چه خوب گفت دینا ناتهر ذیل تاریخبخش
هزار و صد نود و دو بماه رمضان است

١ — عاقبت بتخیر باد فرخنده و همایون باد برب العباد راتم و مصنف ابیات مهتر
دینا ناتهر نوکر سرکاری فیصمدار دروازهٔ سمتِ غرب بر اهتمام محمد پناه
داروغهٔ مرتب یافته بکارسازی

٢ — بهگوان و رو پاگلکاران سنگتراش صورت ترتیب گرفت واقعه بتاریخ یازدهم شهر
ذی الحجهٔ سنهٔ یکهزار و یکصد و نود و دو هجری الهی کرم بمعمورهٔ شهر حفظها
الله

He is eternal.

Wonderfully pure is the society of (this) district of Hindustan!
14

God is always taking care of Padshahpur. By the order of Khan Nazm-ud-din and Badshah Begum, who is bestowing favours on the ryots as well as the poor people.

Under the exalted shelter of that mine of kindness, all the people are enjoying themselves abundantly.

Never (is) there rapine or oppression with regard to anybody.

They are growing spontaneously, earning their bread by way of trade with pleasure.

This fortification is made so perfectly strong that the enemies are running away, struck with awe at it.

Diprap Ram, the accountant, is exerting himself like honest men with a sincere heart.

At evening he is sprinkling gems, like a spring shower, on the artisan and poor labourers.

Be blessed with a thousand years of happiness! All the people are wont to speak thus constantly. How well has Dinanath said in the postscript of its date, —it is the month of Ramzan of the year 1192 (A.H.).

May the end be good and happy and auspicious, through the help of God!

The writer and composer of these couplets (is) Mehta Dinanath, a servant of the Government, (which is) the centre of all favours.

B.—This western gate (was) constructed with the exertion of Mahomed Panah Darogeh ; the design (was) executed by Bhagvan and Rupa, earth workers, stone-cutter.

Dated the 11th of the month of zil-haj, 1192 A.H.

O God! be kind to the population of the town! May God preserve it.

STONE INSCRIPTION OF THE MAUSOLEUM OF BÁLAN SHAH PIR AT KHARAKADI.
Dated A.H. 1245.

Kharakadi is a small village about twelve miles south-west of Bhavnagar. At this village there is a mausoleum of one Sheikh Abu Mahomed Fekeria, who was a very religious man, and who is said to have lived one hundred years, having died in A.H. 666, A.D. 1267-68. The mausoleum was caused to be built by a Mahomedan nobleman in honour of the great Sheikh in A.H. 1245, A.D. 1829-30. The inscription relates to the building of the mausoleum, and is cut into a white sandstone built up in the mausoleum. It contains eight lines in Arabic and is well preserved.

١ — بسم الله الرحمن الرحيم لا اله الا الله محمد رسول الله ٥

٢ — الاانّ اولياء الله ٥ شيخ سيد و ديان از صدق دل سيدنّ

٣ — ذات شد آزاد شد از حق شد و اصل (ابن) شيخ الكبير قطب

٤ — العالم المنير بهاء والحق والشرح والدين ابوالين مسمائي ابو محمد زكريا بن محمد

٥ — غوث بن ابي بكرن القريشي تولد في ليلة الجمعه في شهر رمضان

٦ — ليلة القدر سنه ست وستين و خمس مايه و كان مدة حياته في الدنيا

٧ — مئة سنة ثم ارتحل من دار الفناء الي مقام البقاء بين الظهر والعصر

٨ — في السابع من صفر سنه ست وستين وست مايه الشيخ و نام مادر

٩ — مخدوم صاحب فاطمه بنت عيسي بن شيخ الاسلام والمسلمين غوث

١٠ — الثقلين شيخ محي الدين عبد القادر الحسني وكنيتان گيلاني ميخوانند

١ — بسم الله الرحمن الرحيم الاان اولياء الله

٢ — الخوف عليهم ولاهم يحزنون لا اله الا الله محمد رسول الله

٣ — در سنه دوازده صد چهل و پنج بناي روضه شد

In the name of God, the merciful and compassionate.

There is no god but God ; Mahomed is the prophet of God.

Verily there shall come no fear on those who are the friends of God, neither shall they be grieved.

The great Seyed, who was religious and a sincere Seyed, was freed and united with God.

The great Sheikh, the pole-star of the illuminated world, the splendour of truth, and understanding, and religion, viz., Abvalin, named Abu Mahomed Zekeria, son of Mahomed Gous, son of Abi Bekr Koreshi, who was born on the night of Friday in the month of Ramzan, (on the night the Koran was sent down) (ବଢ଼ଗଏଝଌ) A. H. 566.

He was one hundred years old in this world. He afterwards passed away from this transitory world to the house of eternity in the afternoon of the 7th of Safer, A.H. 666. The Sheikh.

The name of the mother of this nobleman was Fatima, daughter of Isa, son of the Sheikh of Islam and Moslems, the saint of both the worlds, viz., Sheikh Mohiddin Abdul Kader, of the descent of Hasan, surnamed Gillani.

In the name of God, the merciful and compassionate.

Verily there shall come no fear on those who are the friends of God, neither shall they be grieved.

There is no god but God : Mahomed is the prophet of God.

The mausoleum was made in the year 1245.

STONE INSCRIPTION NEAR THE GÂDI GATE AT MÂNGROL.

This inscription is cut into a soft yellow stone with a face of 22″ × 11″ and contains thirteen lines in Persian. The stone is built up in the wall near the Gâdi Gate at Mângrol. It contains an order by Prince Azam Khan to the Governors not to oppress the people. Though there is no date, it appears to have been written soon after the death of Emperor Aurangzeb, when Prince Azam, his second son, held the sway for a short time in opposition to his brother, afterwards Emperor Bahadur Shah of Delhi.

---

1 ــ در عهد بادشاه روي زمين ناصر

2 ــ الدنيا والدين ابوالفتح احمد شاه سلطان

3 ــ كه احداث نامشروع از وقت كفار باز در

4 ــ قصبهٔ منگلور (وجور واربسمئي) بنام بعضي زميندار

5 ــ تعيين بود چون شاهزاده اعظم فتحخان مد الله عمره

6 ــ براي فتح قلعهٔ گرنال عزيمت فرمودند كيفيت

7 ــ احداث مذكور ملك علاء سهراب و صوفي دكن

8 ــ وهمير هرراج و جيسا مينه قصر با مهاجن محدود

9 ــ در سمع بندگي خان اعظم بازنمودند اشارت

10 ــ شد تا بر وفق التماس كاركنان پروانه

11 ــ كرده دهند تا بعد ازين تاريخ در گرد اينچنين

12 ــ نامشروع نگردند بر حكم پروانه روند × × × ×

× × × × × × × × ×

× × × ×

In the reign of Ahmedshah Sultan, the king of the world, the defender of the faith and the world, the father of victory.

Certain illegal pollutions of the time of the infidels were again committed in the names of several zamindars in the town of Mânglore (Mângrol).

When Shaha Zadeh (Prince) Azam Fatteh Khan went to conquer the fortress of Girnal, they having brought to the ears of Khan Azim the account of the above said illegalities of *Malik Ala Şohrab*, * Hamir Hari Raj and Jesasing, in connection with the Mahjan ; it was ordered that in accordance with the request the karkuns should issue a parvanch (પરવાનો), so that the people, abstaining in future from such illegality, should follow the parvanch.

STONE INSCRIPTION OF THE JUMA MUSJID AT DELAVÂDÂ.
Dated A.H. 1291.

This inscription is cut into a white marble, which is built up in the eastern wall of the mosque at Delavâdâ, a small town to the north of the Portuguese possession of Diu on the south coast of Kâthiâvâd. It is of a very recent date, as it mentions the building of the mosque by Navab Mohobat Khan of Junâgâdh in A.H. 1291, A.D. 1874. It is written in five lines in Persian within a space of 14″ × 11″.

يا فتاح

1 — ز نواب مهابت خان فلك جاه

2 — چه رسم خضر از نزهت ادا شد

3 — ز روئی شكر خلق عام گفت اين

4 — خدا را ز والي سورَّم بنا شد

۱۲   ۹۰

مطرح   مطرح   مطرح

O ! The Opener !

From *Nawab Mohobat Khan*, the pomp of sky, what a Khizr-like duty is performed with purity ! By way of thanks-giving the people in general said that this was made for God by the Governor of Soreth, 1290.

15

www.ingramcontent.com/pod-product-compliance
Lightning Source LLC
Chambersburg PA
CBHW022027080426
42733CB00007B/754